Steampunk Cats Drawing

A Completely New Form of Cats

By Jeffrey Stains

Table of Contents

Disclaimer

While all attempts have been made to verify the information provided in this book, the author does assume any responsibility for errors, omissions, or contrary interpretations of the subject matter contained within. The information provided in this book is for educational and entertainment purposes only. The reader is responsible for his or her own actions and the author does not accept any responsibilities for any liabilities or damages, real or perceived, resulting from the use of this information.

The trademarks that are used are without any consent, and the publication of the trademark is without permission or backing by the trademark owner. All trademarks and brands within this book are for clarifying purposes only and are the owned by the owners themselves, not affiliated with this document.

Introduction

"Steampunk Cats Drawing-A Completely New Form of Cats" is a completely new form of cats. You might have seen different animals in the Steampunk genre of art. But, the tutorials given in this book are a completely new set of instructions that you would have never encountered before. This book is designed keeping in mind those artists who might have touched a few chords of Steampunk genre, but want to explore completely new arenas of art. Steampunk is a widespread art form that encompasses literally anything and everything from the current world as well as from the ancient globe.

You might have read our previous books on Steampunk. But, in case you have not gone through them, you do not need to worry. This book is a complete set of instructions in itself. You will not feel at any point in the chapters that you are missing something.

Steampunk genre actually belongs to the setting of the Victorian era. The mainstream artists of our age took inspiration from the steam engines of that age and incorporated the same in the modern day gadgets like mobile phones, tablets and the airplanes etc.

In the first part of this book, you will find a brief introduction about the cats depicted in the paintings in the last couple of centuries. The initial introduction is written to make you familiar with the art forms of cats in the past. Cats have been a subject of many forms of art in literally every field. They are a part of our lives as pets, as stray animals, etc. Thus, this book is in a way inspired from the widespread presence of cats and kittens in our lives.

In the second section, you will find the tutorials based on Steampunk drawings of cats. The tutorials are given in a step by step manner so that you can pick up any illustration from the middle of the book and just sit down to draw. We would recommend that you practice a few drawings of cats and that of machine parts separately if you are an amateur at the genre of Steampunk. This would help you to get your hands on the illustrations mentioned in the book relatively easily.

Enjoy exploring one more aspect of this fascinating genre.

Section 1
Cats in Art

Before drawing Steampunk cats, you must be aware of drawing normal sketches of cats. Practice a few drawings of cats in various positions and with different expressions. You must be thinking how can you give expressions in an animal? But, the fact is that animals do express their emotions by different expressions of face. Internet is full of pictures these days which reveal extremely beautiful expressions of animals like squirrels, dogs, cats, horses, etc. You can pick any picture of a cat and try drawing it in different mediums. Charcoal is a very beautiful medium for drawing anything on a piece of paper. They also come in many gradations of hues.

Cat is a very flexible feline, which has been a subject of paintings in past and present. They are also depicted in the subplots of paintings. An important reason for choosing cats as a subject of paintings is the love of Americans for the cute animal. They are found in abundance in the households of people all over the world. That is why this feline has mushroomed in art in various forms over the centuries.

Cats in paintings of artists

Leonardo da Vinci once wrote, "The smallest feline is a masterpiece". He had a great admiration for the flexibility of cats. Many other artists like Paul Gauguin and Thomas Gainsborough also studied and observed cats. In the Victorian era, the cats became the cuddly members familiar to females in the paintings. Edouard Manet painted cat in the lap of his sweet niece Julie in 1887. A black cat painted by Manet in the painting Olympia is somewhat less assuring. Some people regard it as the symbol of female prostitution because it was perched on the bed of a naked woman. This painting had scandalized the city of Paris when it was exhibited in 1865.

There are some benign paintings by many artists. "Cat Catching a Bird" by Picasso, "Fritz the Cat" by Robert Crumba are some of the examples of such paintings. "The Cook and the Cat" by Théodule-Augustin Ribot depicts a hungry cat secretly grabbing a fish lying beside a cook in the kitchen. The cook seemed oblivious to the cat or he might have decided to overlook the act of his four-legged buddy. The anthropomorphic painting of a cat by Louis Wain is abstract and increasingly hallucinatory. Some people say that his schizophrenia was responsible for this strange painting.

Similarly, another interesting painting is "The Bridge" by a Swedish artist Carl Olof Larsson made in 1920. The painting's focal point is the silhouette like figure of a cat, which is sitting beside her mistress, who is painting a bridge in the garden. The lady and the cat are peering at the man who just came on the bridge and disrupted the painting of the mistress, who had come to the garden to paint the beautiful bridge in complete solitude. As you will notice in this painting, it is not necessary to paint the feline with complete details all the time. Sometimes, just a hint of shadow is enough to convey your idea.

Cats in Steampunk

When you see the Steampunk drawings of cats in the following chapters, you will notice that we have illustrated many drawings of cats in different positions. Various mechanical parts are used in the drawings. You can take the help of classical paintings from the previous centuries. Alternatively, you can take references from the internet to turn any drawing of a cat into a Steampunk cat.

In this book, you will not find any lessons on how to draw a cat. Instead, you will be directed about drawing Steampunk cats. Cats speak their own language. When you draw these Steampunk drawings of cats, you will find that each figure of the feline is in one way similar, yet different from each other. Let us begin.

Section 2

Chapter 1 - Cat Drawing 1

Step 1

Draw the circular outline of the face of a cat. Draw the triangular tip carefully because the pinky area of the nose is a crucial part in the drawing. Give a slight hint of the mouth as well. Notice that the lines for the eyes are made slightly tapering towards the corners.

All these lines will serve as guides for drawing the remaining face accurately.

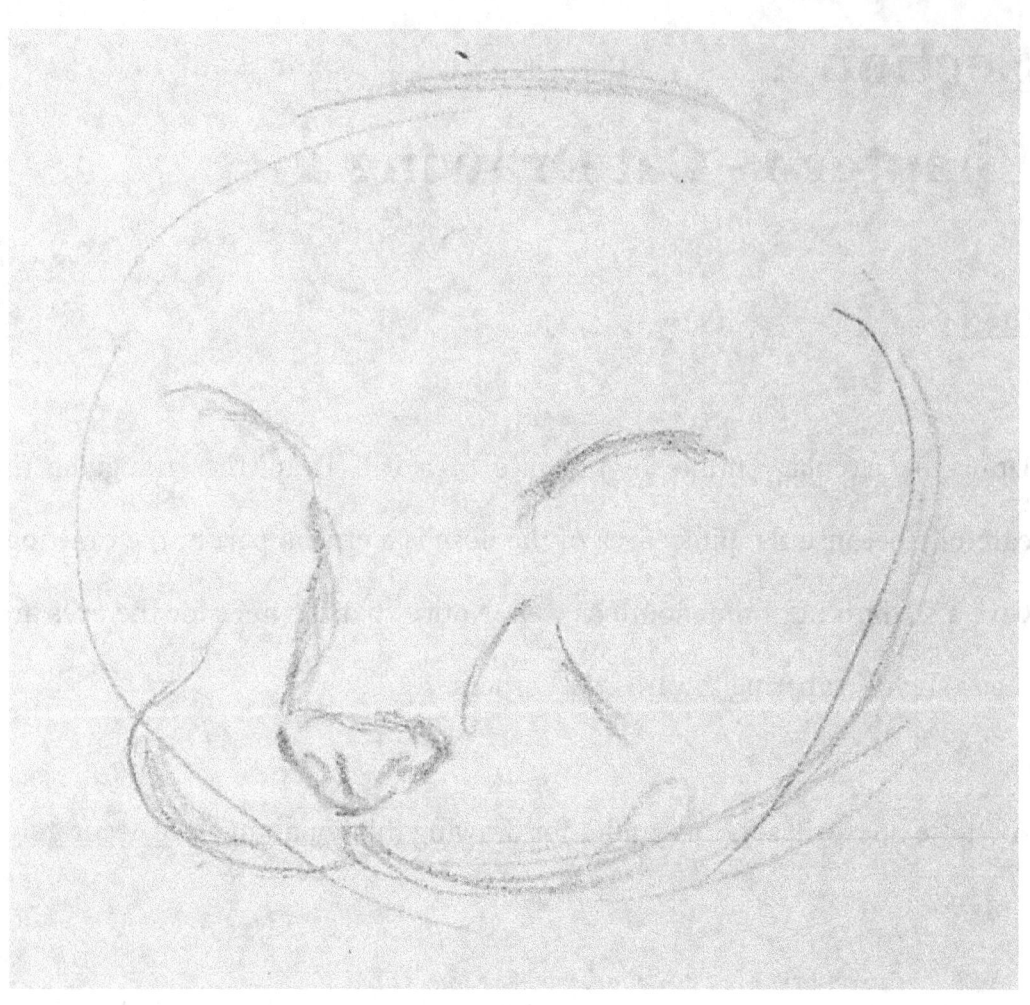

Step 2

Draw the outline of the eyes and the eye balls completely. The pointed ears are protruding in both directions. The nose and mouth are given slight details in this step.

The cat is given a heavy body in the end. That is why we have used open curved lined to suggest the presence of chubby skin on the body.

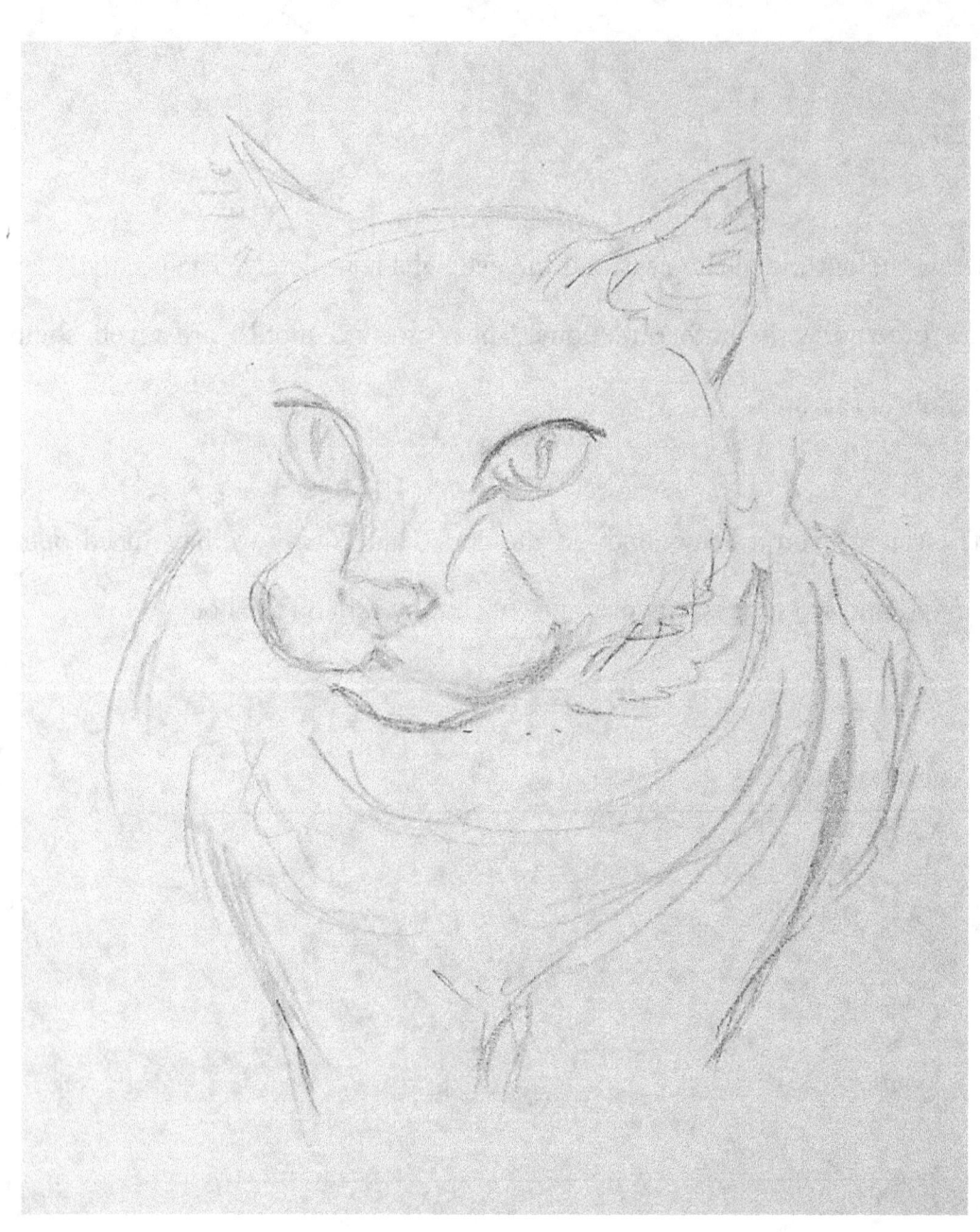

Step 3

Draw a hat on the head of the cat. On this hat, give a suggestion of the outline of swimming glasses. But, do not give the inner details of the glasses because we will convert these glasses into two clocks later. Join the two circles of the swimming glasses with a thick belt or a shaft.

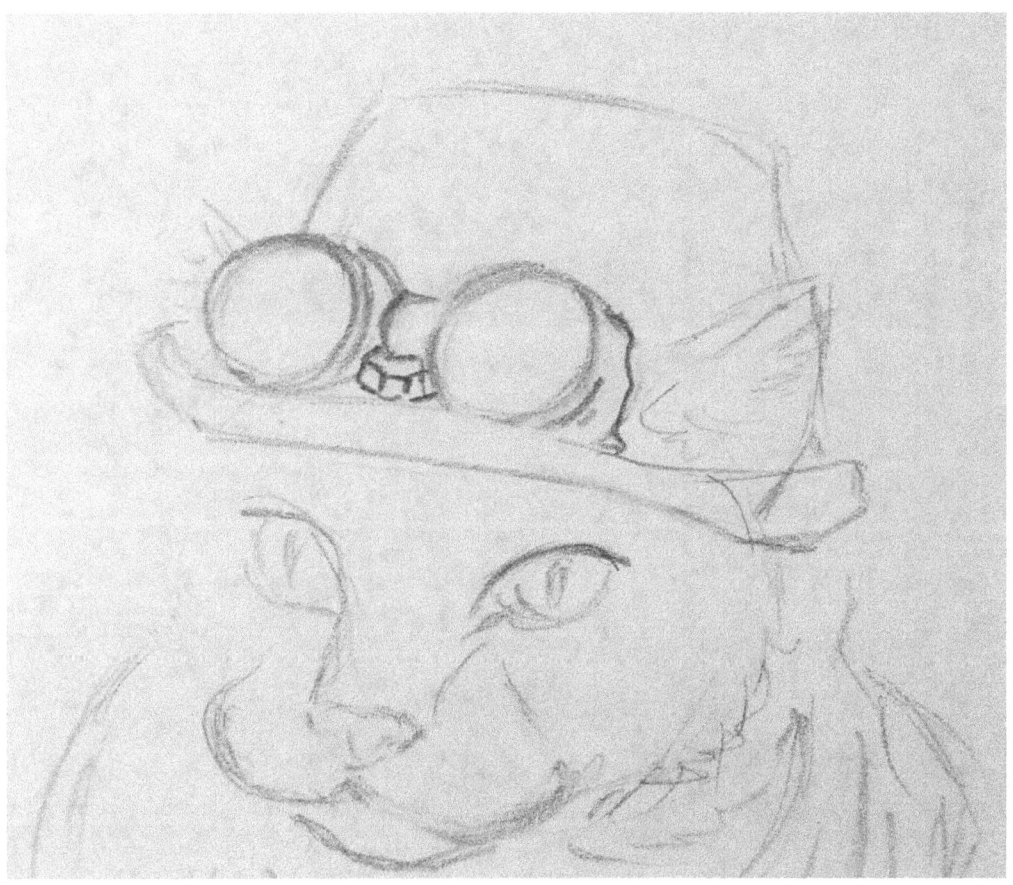

Step 4

Draw the hands of clock in both the clocks placed on the hat. The clock is not made in a regular fashion. It looks like the ancient clock of the Victorian era. There are two arrow hands in both the clock. One thinner arrow hand is inserted in the left clock. And the right clock consists of one thin hand with a ball at the tip.

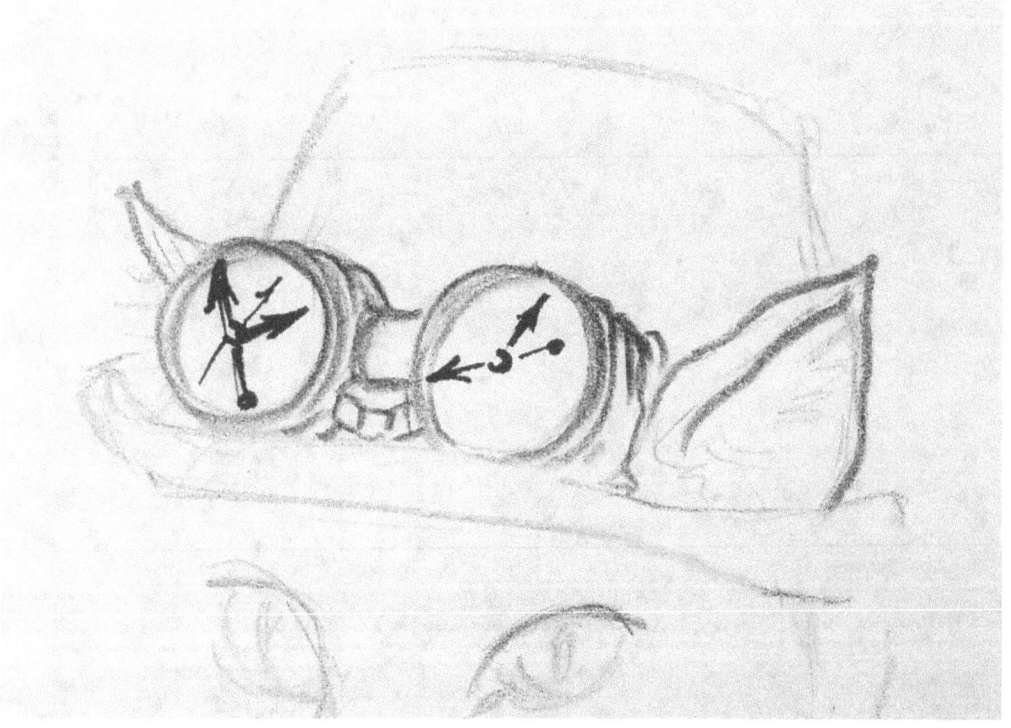

Step 5

Thicken the outline of the hat. The base line of the hat is given prominence. Draw a chain beginning from the top right corner of the hat. The beginning portion of the hat is the knob like thing from which the chain is emerging. The links of the chain are drawn precisely so that it looks a little realistic.

The end of the chain consists of a key. This key might be the second half of the lock of a secret treasure. You never know, this cat might be the animal transformation of the guard of that treasure! Wink!

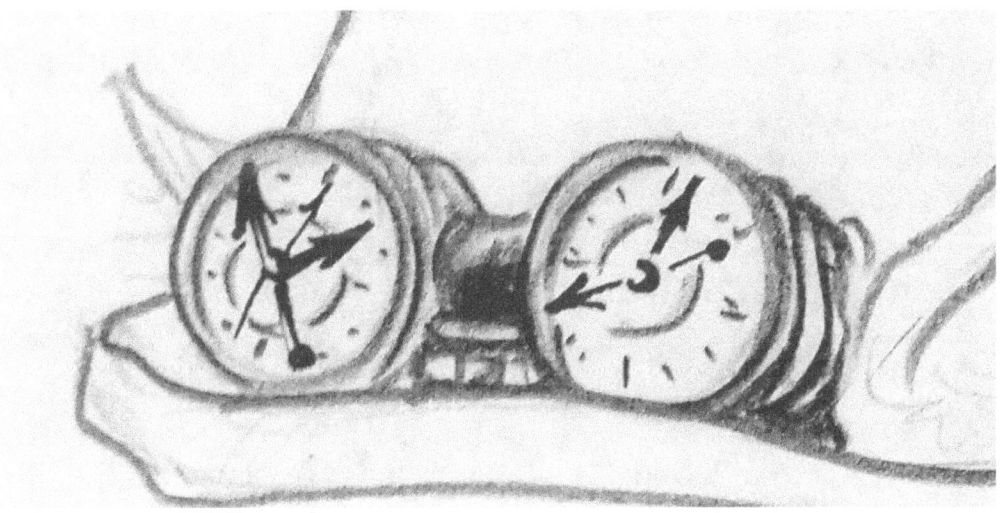

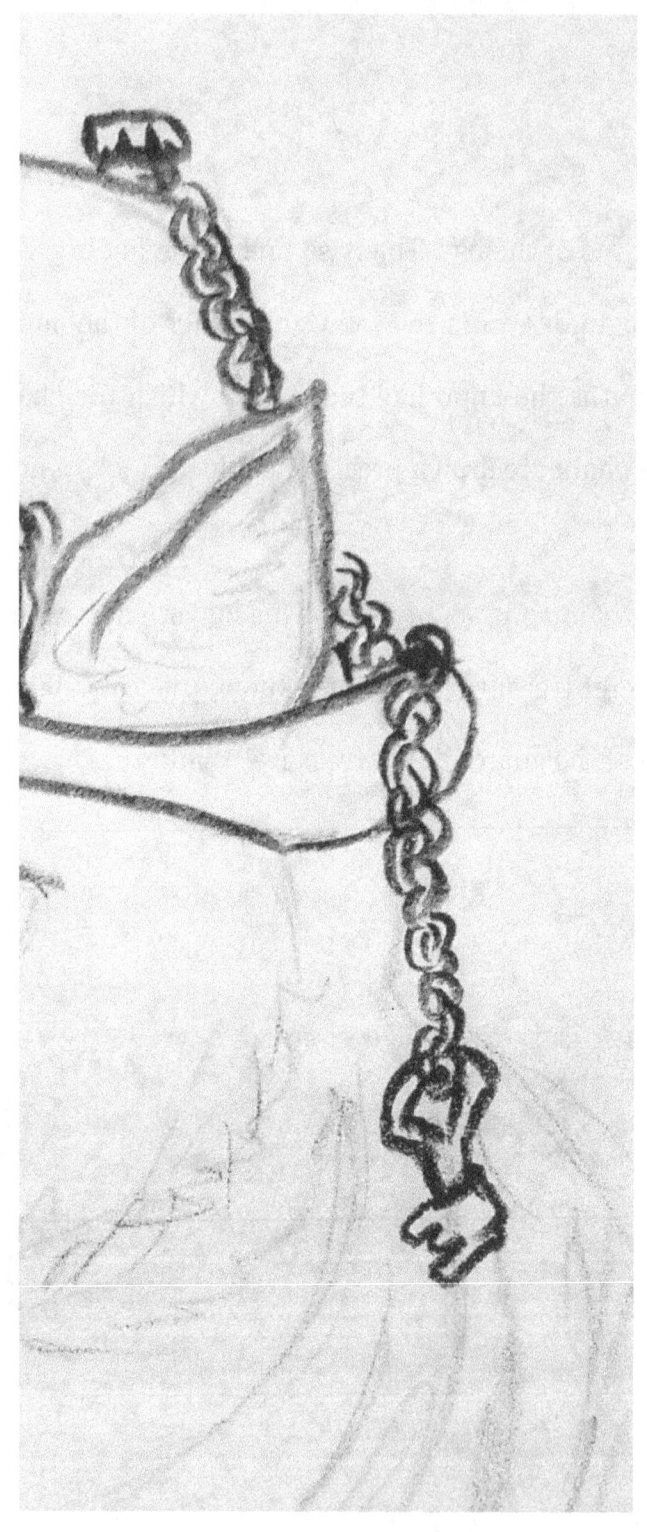

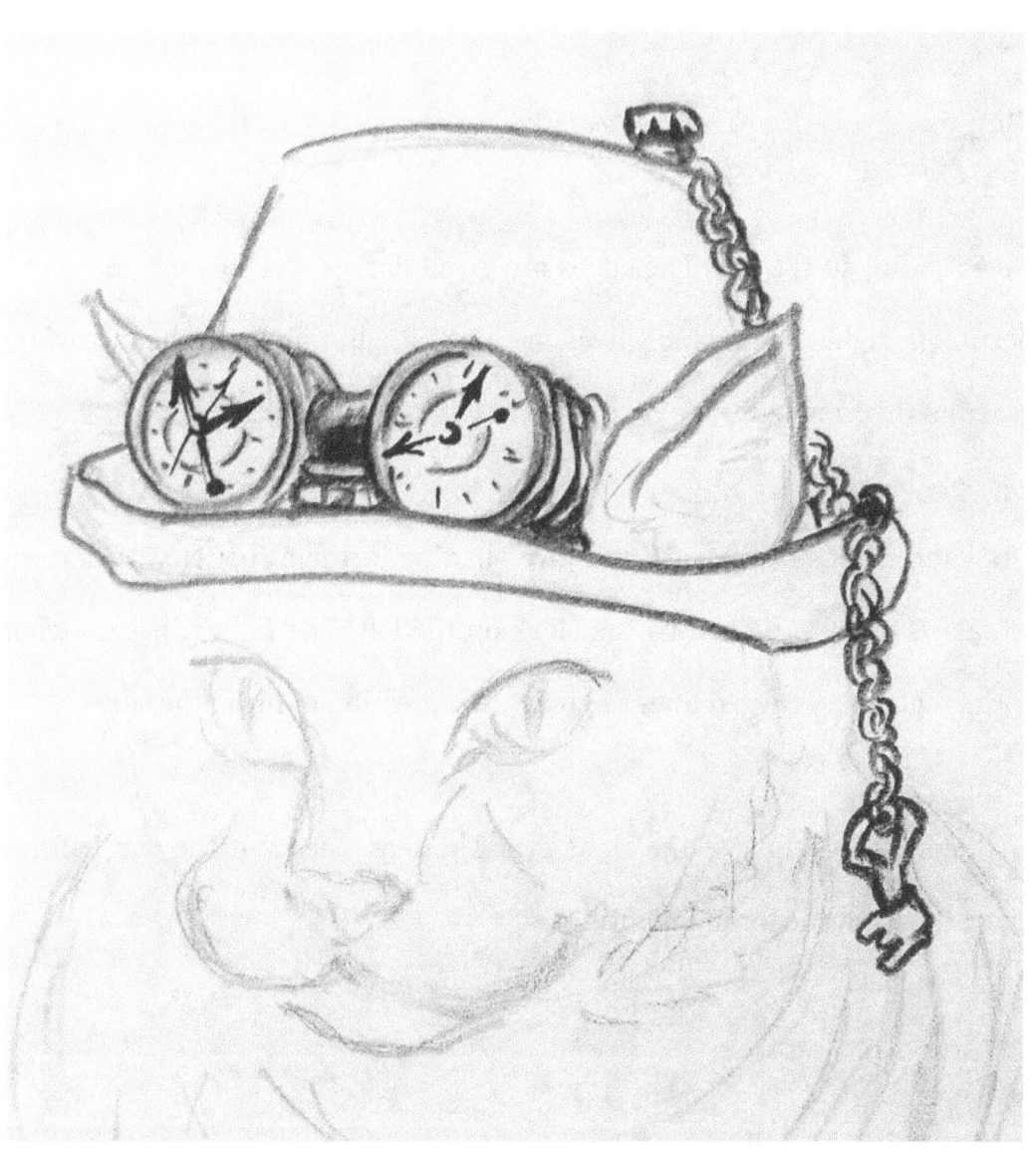

Step 6

Give shading in the hat. The edges are given darker shading and the center portion is highlighted, which gives the idea of light falling on the face of the cat from the front.

Draw the details of the ears and give shading in them too. Notice that the left ear is majorly hidden by the clock on the left. The right ear is sketched with tangled and rugged lines to give the impression of fur in the ear.

Highlight the outline of the right eye. The tear duct and the eye ball are given thick outline for highlighting.

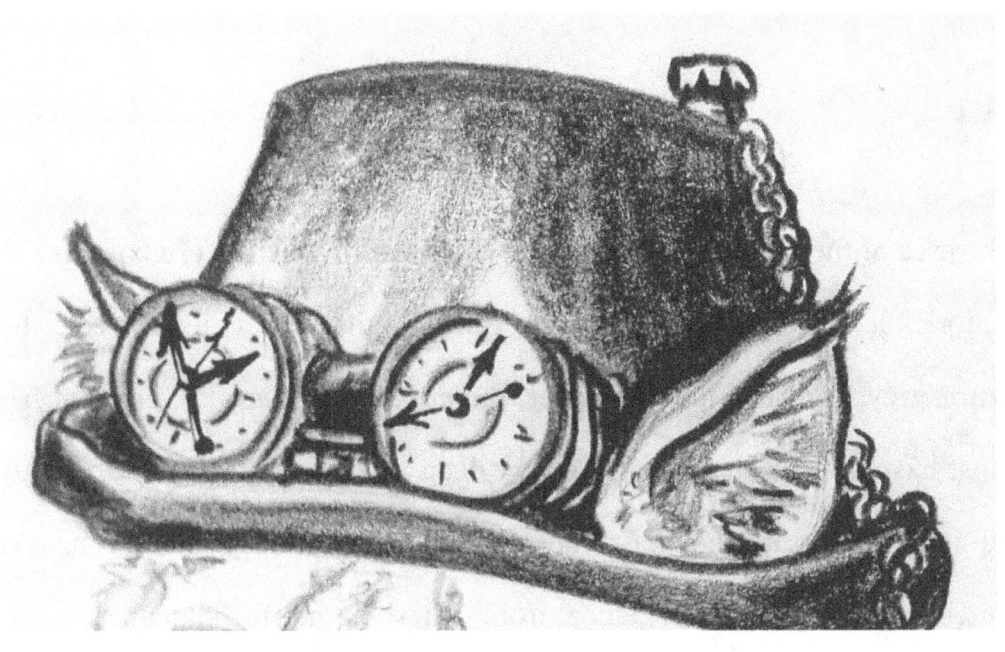

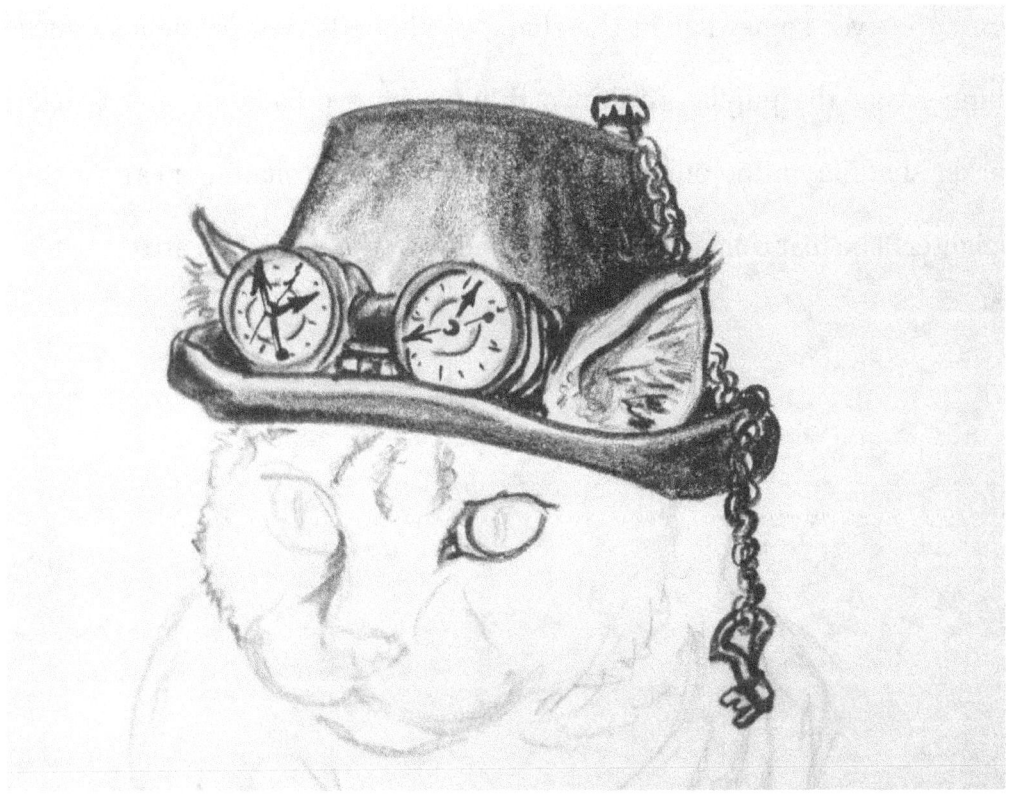

Step 7

The eyes of the feline have a glitter in their eyes. And their eye balls are not majorly black or brown like humans. The eye balls are very light in color like azure, grey, and sky blue. Moreover, the pupil is also usually very thin. You must have noticed that cats have very deep and intriguing eyes, which give the impression that they have the capability to look deep inside your soul. And sometimes, they steal glances from you when they feel hideous.

Draw the eyes somewhat in the shape of almonds. Shade them in such a manner that the pupils are drawn thinly. The eye balls are given slightly darker shading on the outer edges is darker and the shading near the pupil is lighter. The tear duct is also highlighted with the help of an arc.

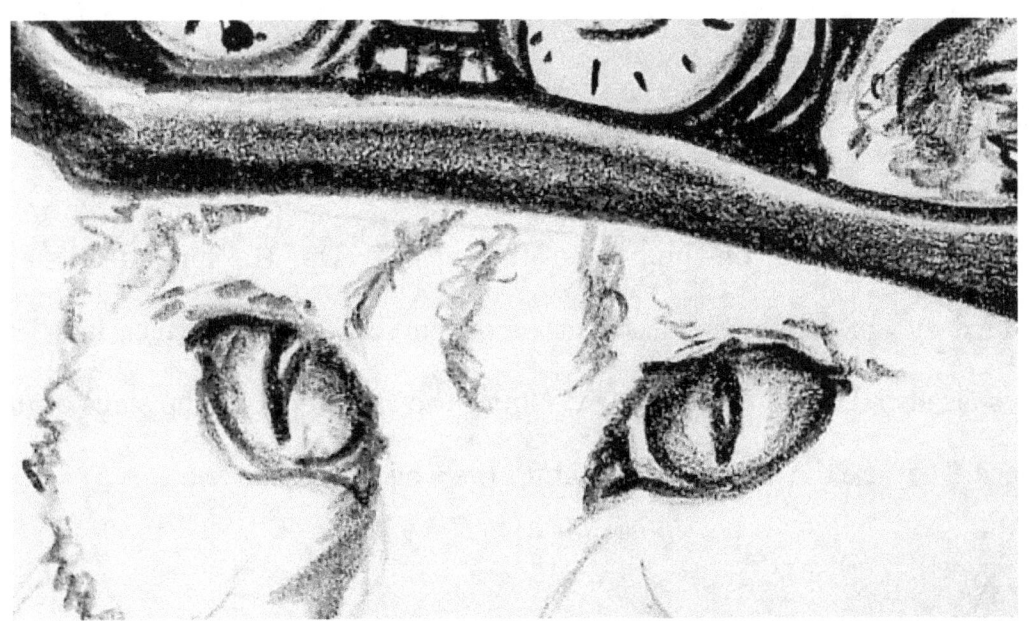

Step 8

In this step, the fur on the body of the cat is drawn. The furry details are added with the help of small strokes on the curves we had drawn earlier. The nose is also drawn more precisely. Notice the small dots on the sides of the nose. They are the originating point for the whiskers of the feline.

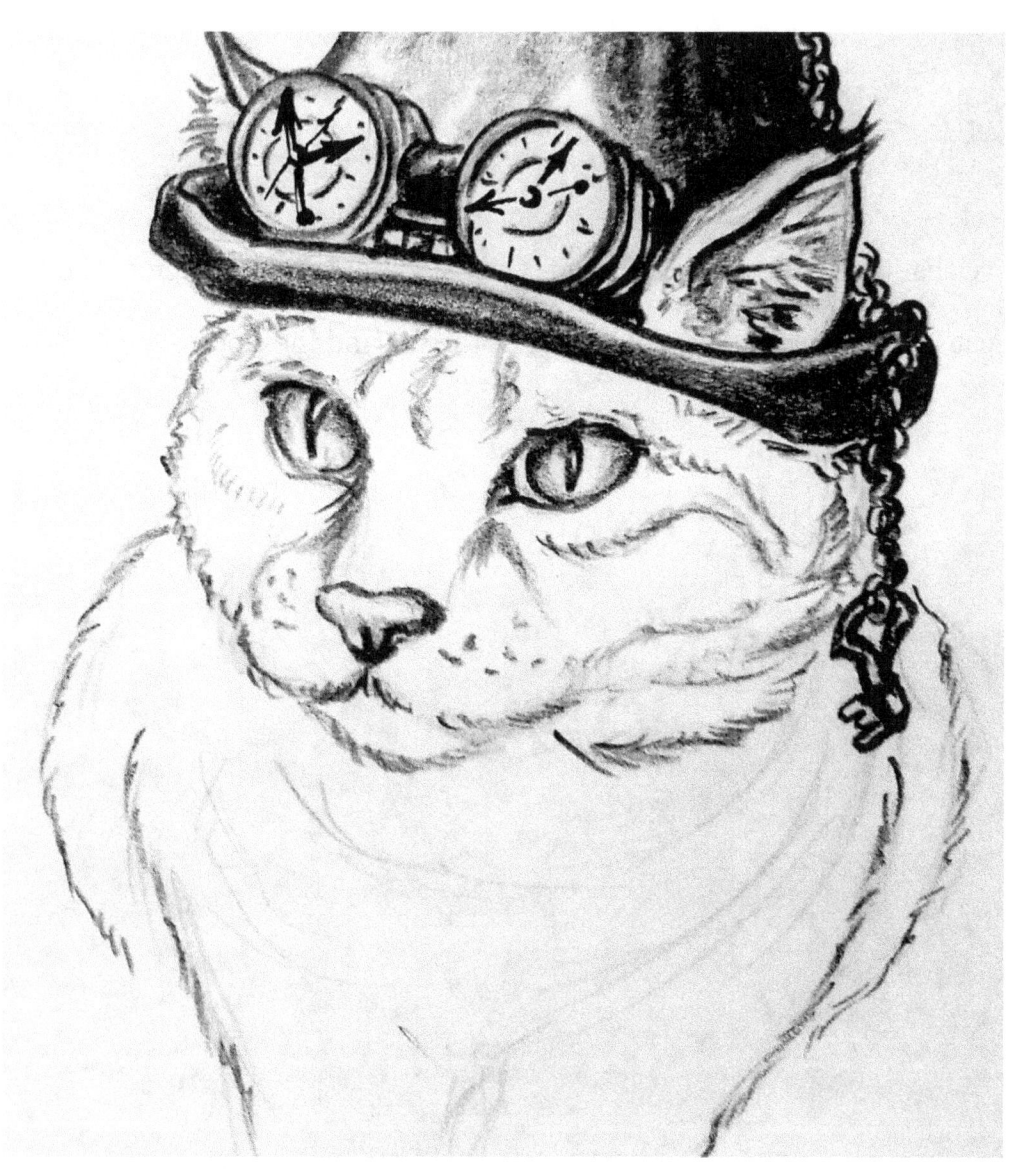

Step 9

Give shading to the body of the cat. Only slight shading is given to the body because the main highlight of this cat is the hat and the clocks.

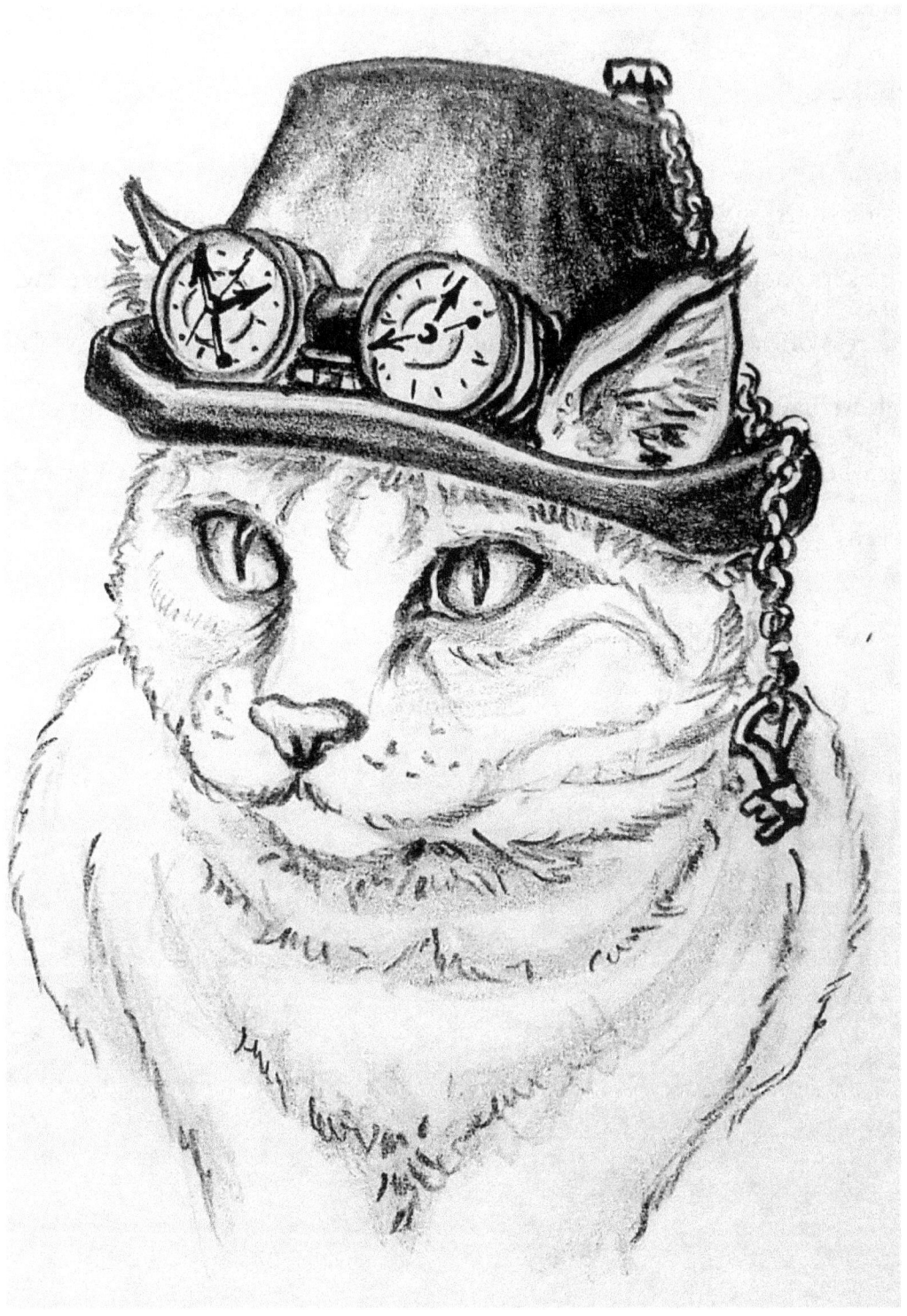

Step 10

Using sharp, single strokes; draw the whiskers on the mouth of the cat. The whiskers should be drawn at the end only so that they do not get mixed with the rest of the drawing and shading. Notice that just below the base of the hat, we have drawn some small strokes which signify the crushed fur of the cat when it wore the hat. In addition, some longer hairs are drawn over the eyes.

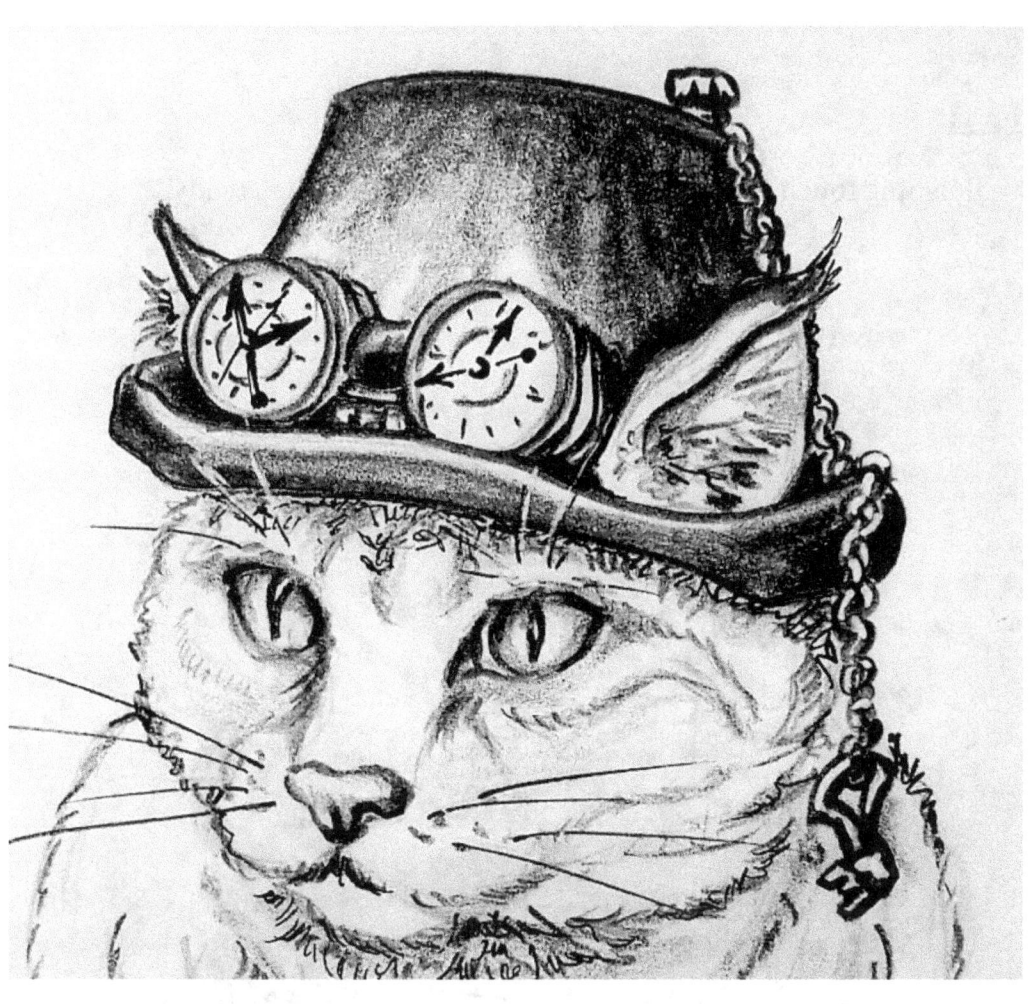

Step 11

Give finishing touch to the feline and the Steampunk cat is ready.

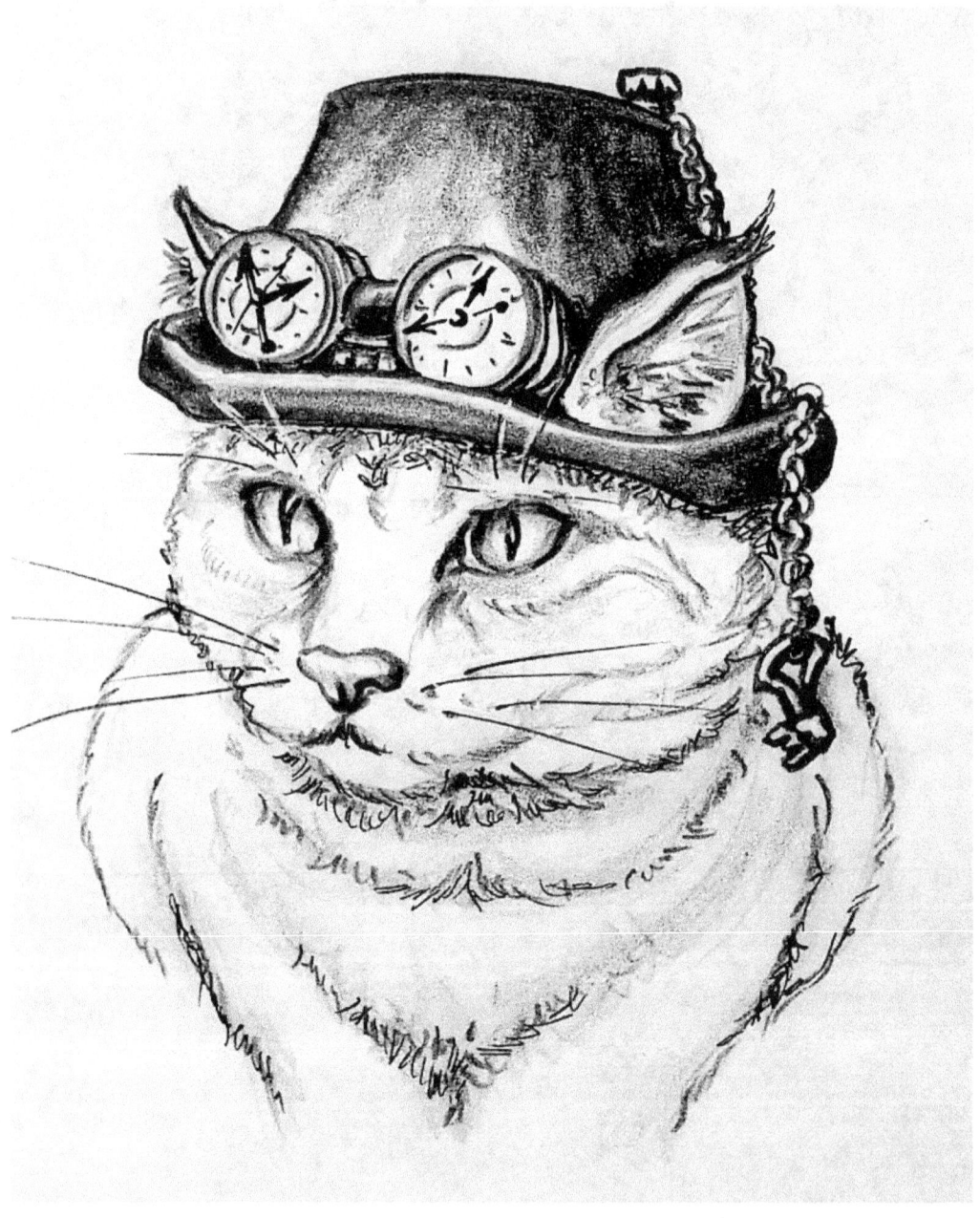

Chapter 2 - Cat Drawing 2

Step 1

Draw the outline of front profile of the cat. We have placed a hat on the head of the cat in this figure also. draw the ears protruding out of the hat. But, the right ear is partially hidden due to the slight turn of the face and somewhat because of the hat.

The furry texture of the face is also given a start in step 1 only. Also, give the outlines of the eyes, nose and mouth.

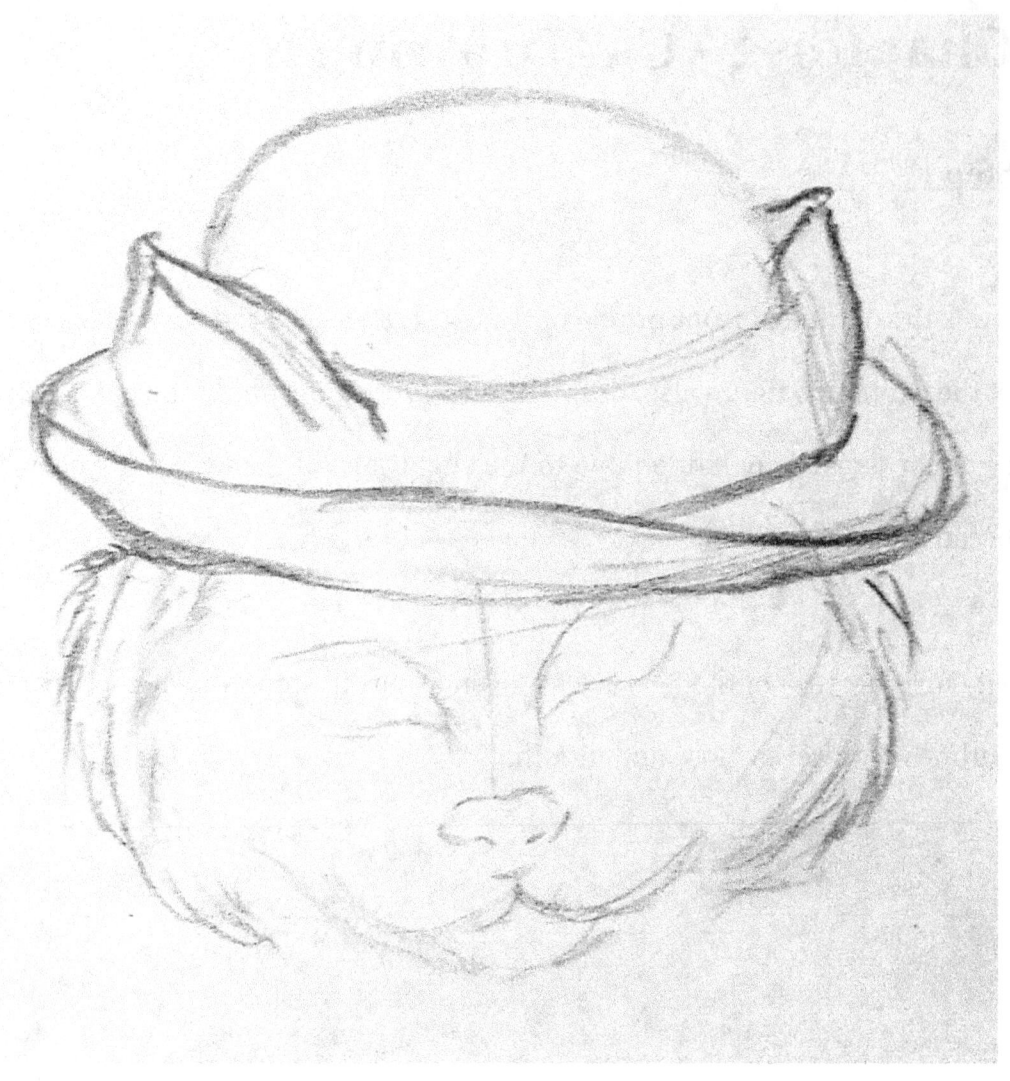

Step 2

Just like we draw a ribbon and a bow on a hat, similarly we have to draw a gear in place of the bow and a strip of fasteners in place of ribbon. A curved strip of fasteners is also drawn at the base of left ear. Draw a large circle with light pencil covering the left eye and a wire emerging from this circle. This circle will serve as a guide for the magnifying lens we will draw later.

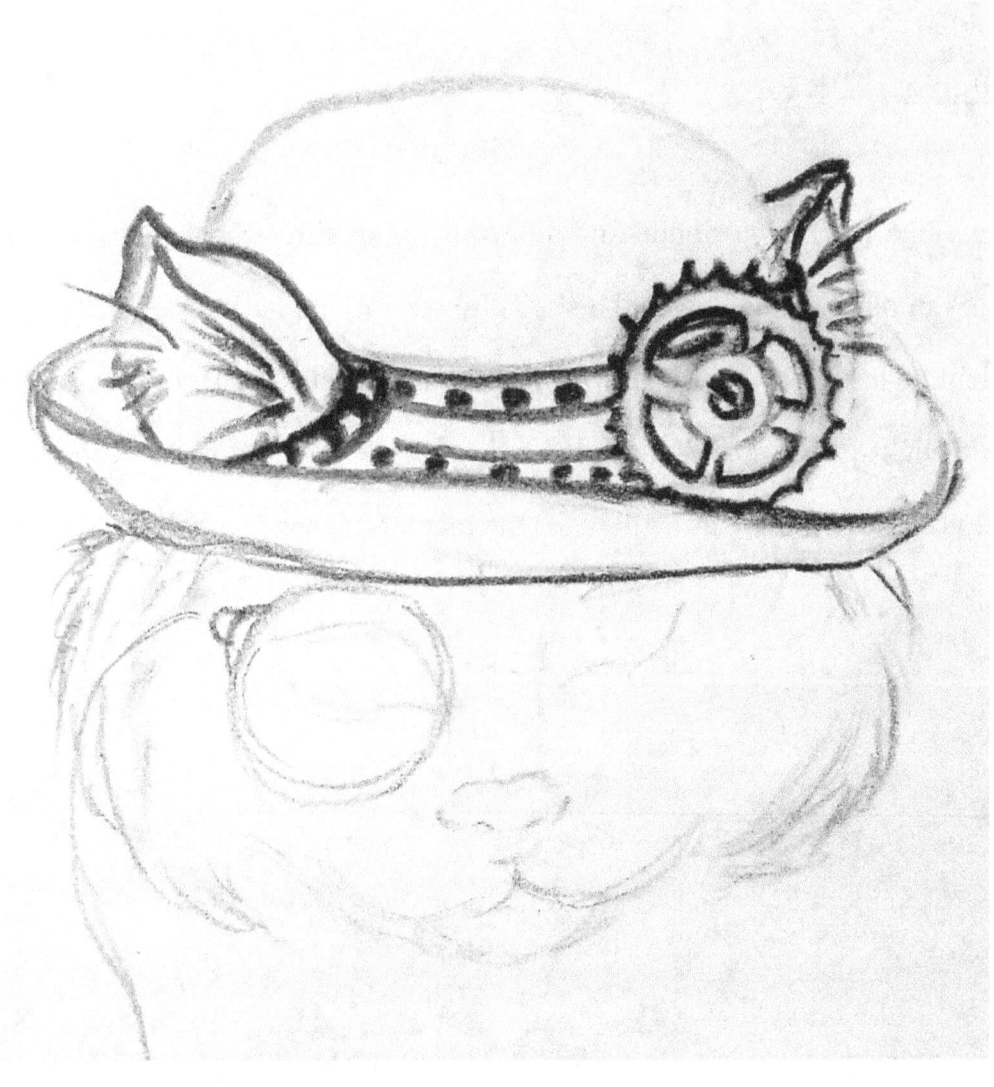

Step 3

Give shading in the hat. The shading is given depth near the small gear. Draw the details of both the ears. Somewhat longer hairs are also emerging outwards from the ears.

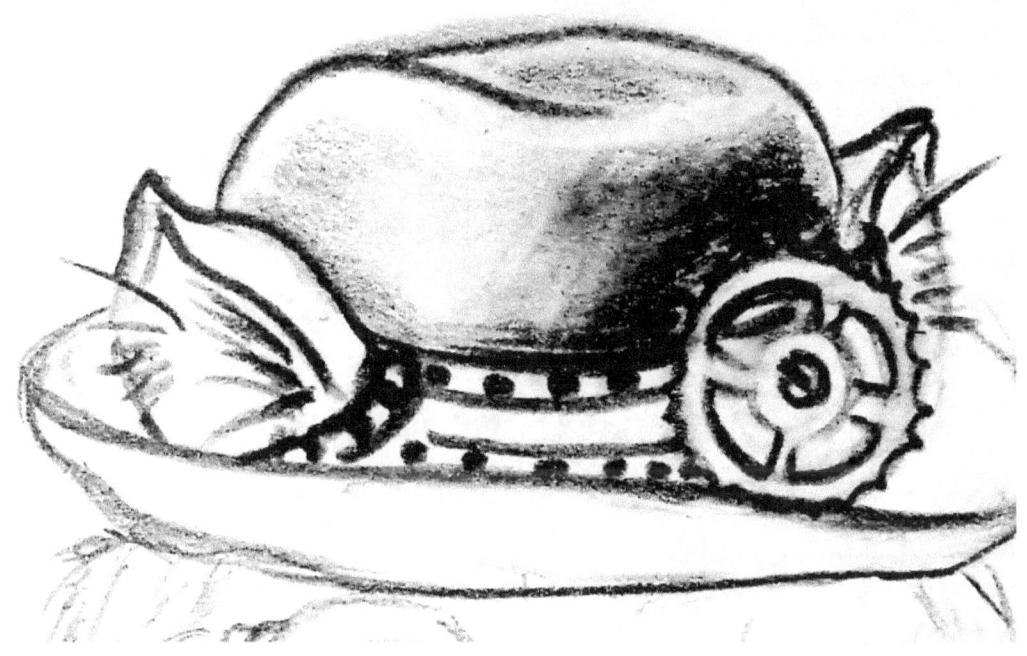

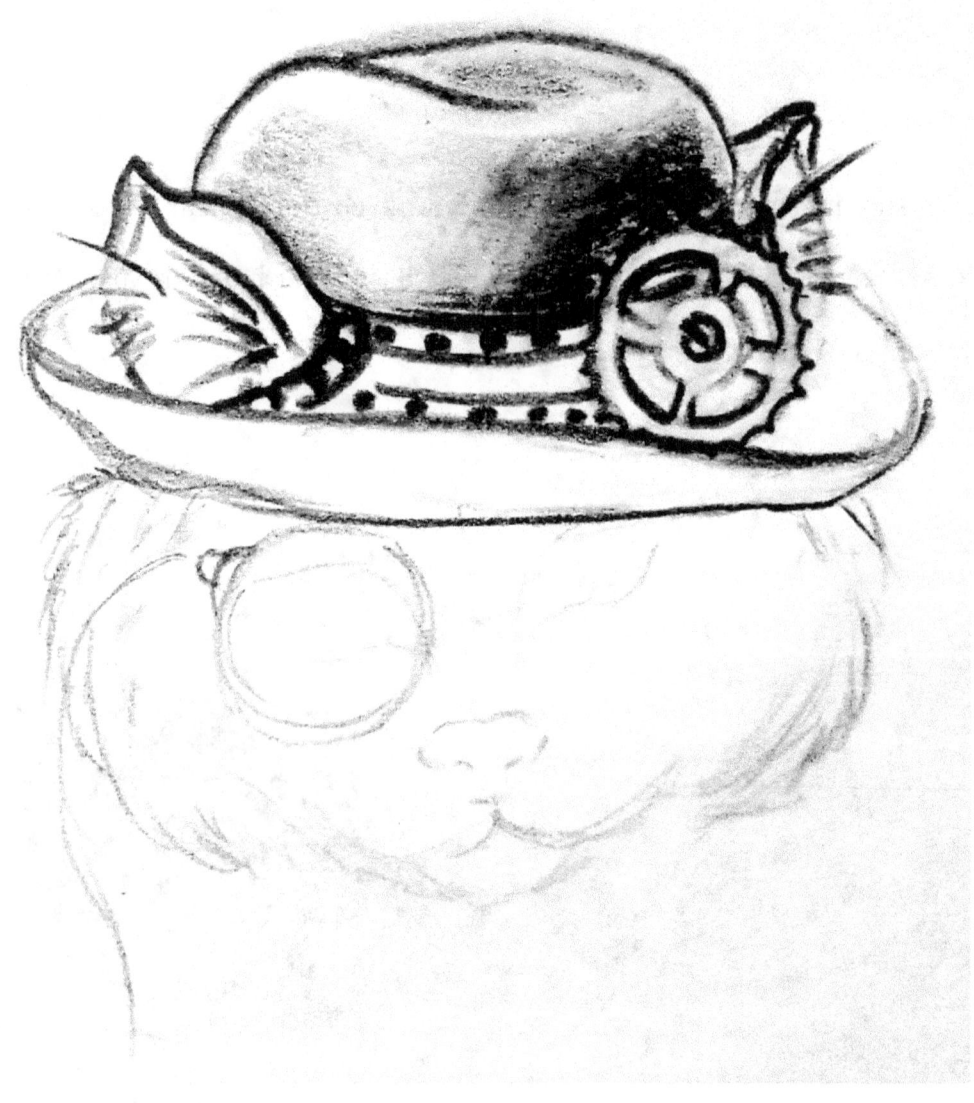

Step 4

Darken the shading in the base of the hat. Notice the change in gradation that depicts the reflection of light. The edge of the hat along the right ear is shaded very lightly.

Give details to the gear and the strip of fasteners. The gaps along the spokes of gear are given darker shading to convey the idea of depth.

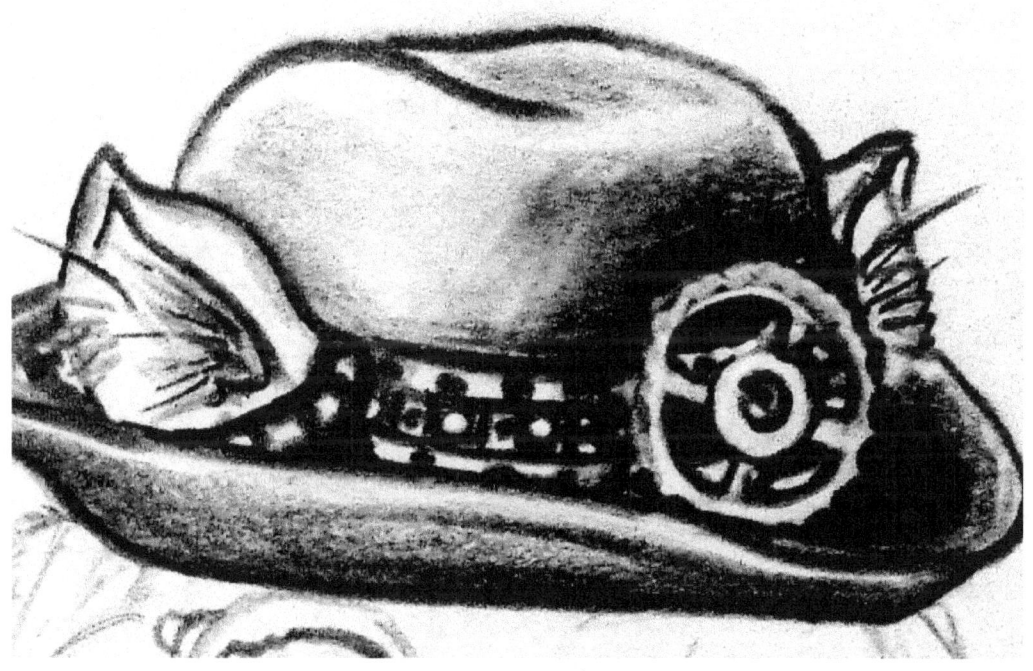

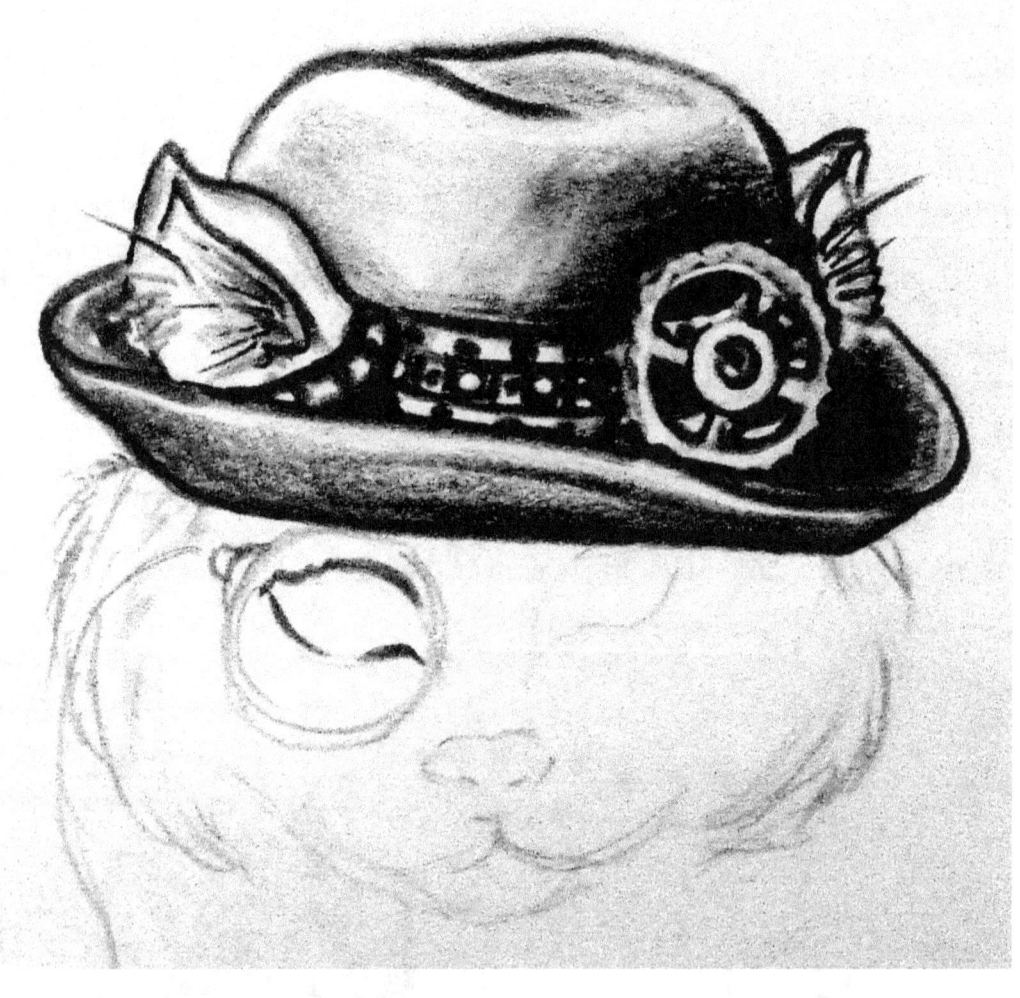

Step 5

We will draw the left eye in this step. You might assume that you do not have to be very careful while drawing the eye behind the magnifying lens, but the fact is that you cannot draw this eye carelessly. Though the magnifying lens is covering the eye, but still, the suggestion of a cat's eye is given precisely. If you try to shade this area with less precision, you might end up messing up the portion.

Thus, firstly draw the outer edge of the lens with two concentric circles. Now give the suggestion of the eye behind the lens. The glassy texture of the lens has been achieved by merging the shading a little with a rag or index finger. The chain emerging from the lens is connected with two knobs placed over each other.

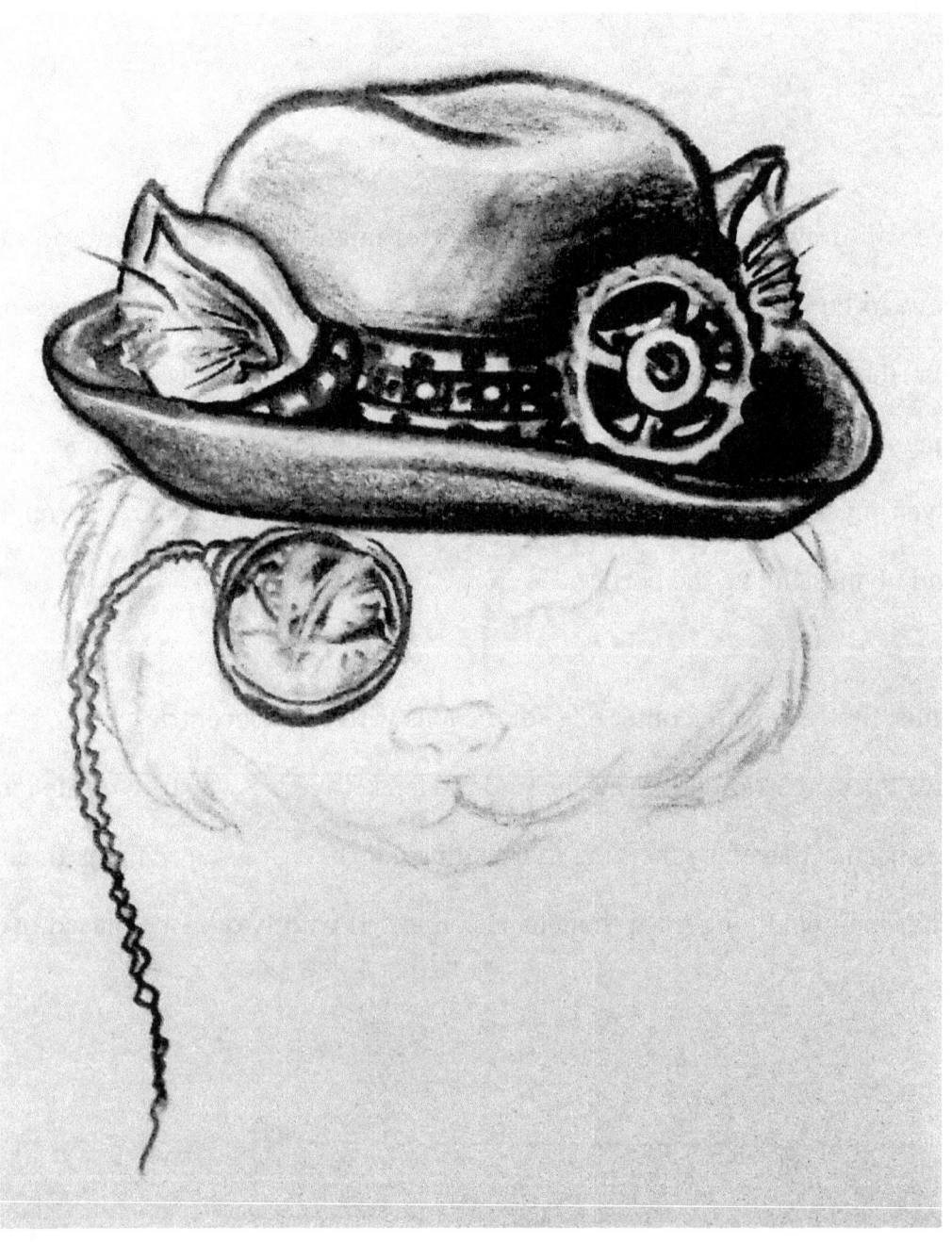

Step 6

Draw the right eye of the animal. In this figure as well, we will draw the pupil like a thin line in the iris. The tear duct is extended downwards in a little exaggerated manner.

Draw the details in the nose. The shine on the tip of the nose is achieved by leaving the space blank.

Also, give the furry details on the body by drawing small strokes of lines. The outward small lines give the suggestion of fur on the body of the cat.

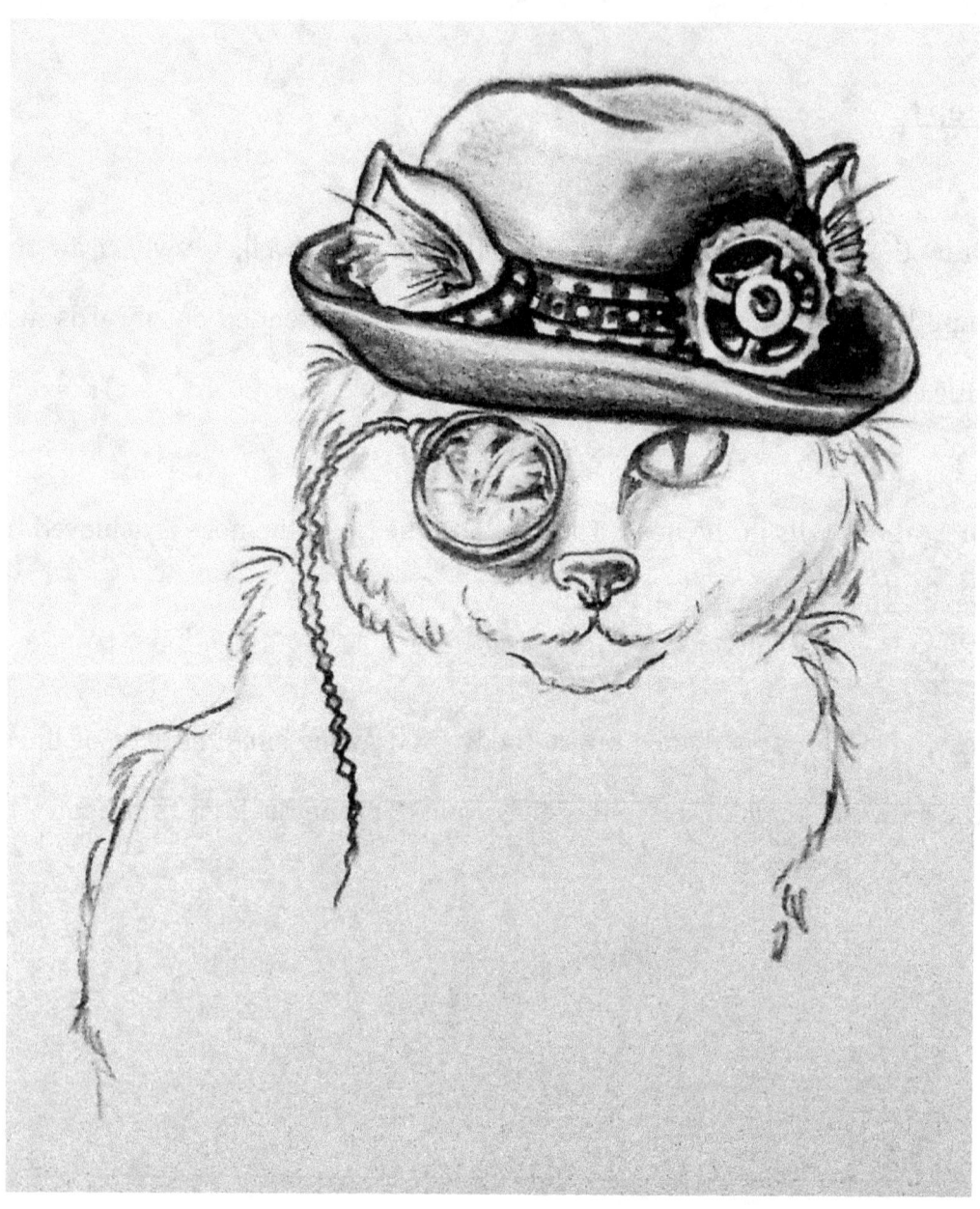

Step 7

Give the details of the fur below the chin. This portion of the fur is drawn like a cravat. It is a little bulging out in style. Draw the fur with small and long lines on conjunction with each other.

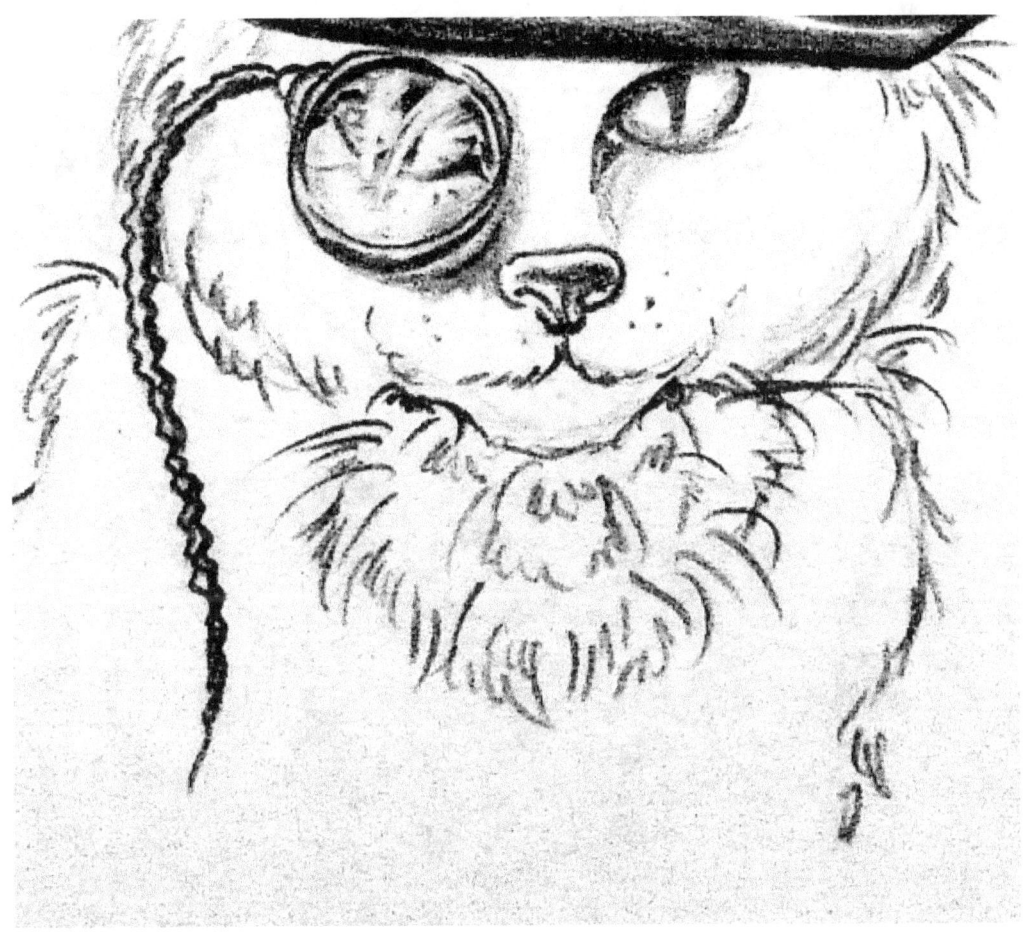

Step 8

With long, single strokes; draw the whiskers protruding from the mouth. As we did in the previous chapter, the whiskers are drawn in the last step only.

Give finishing touch to the sketch. Your Steampunk pirate cat is ready.

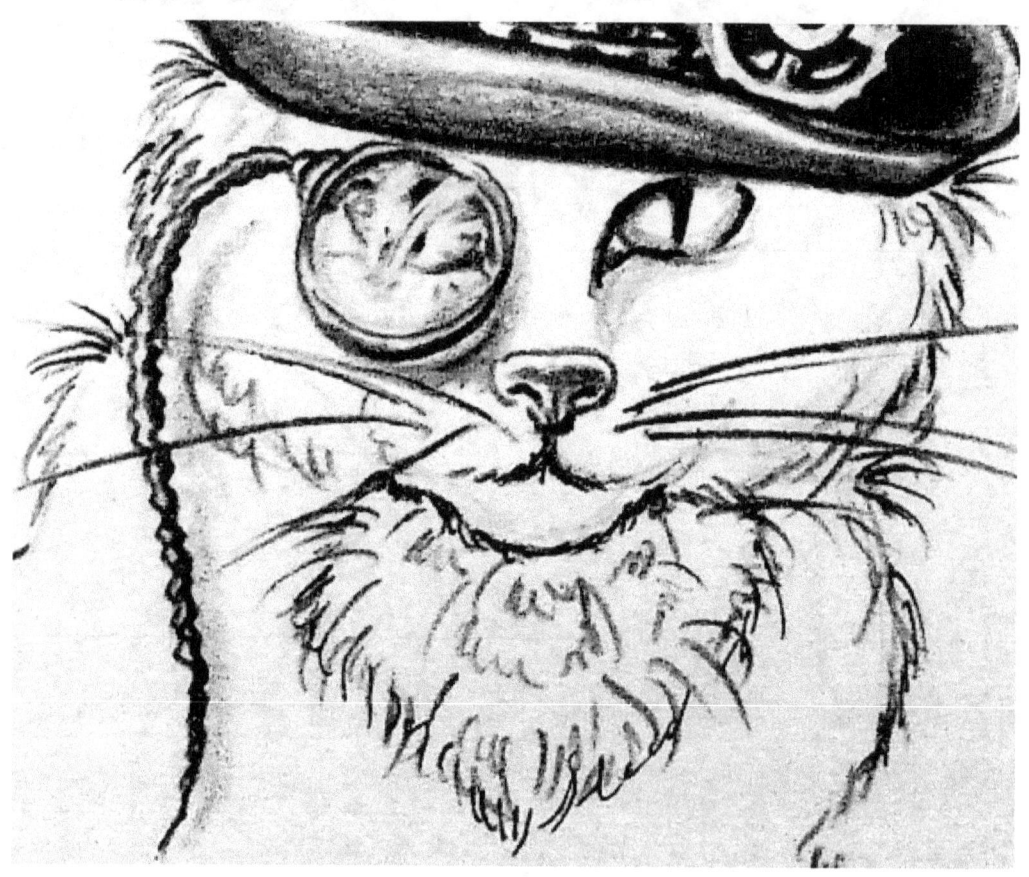

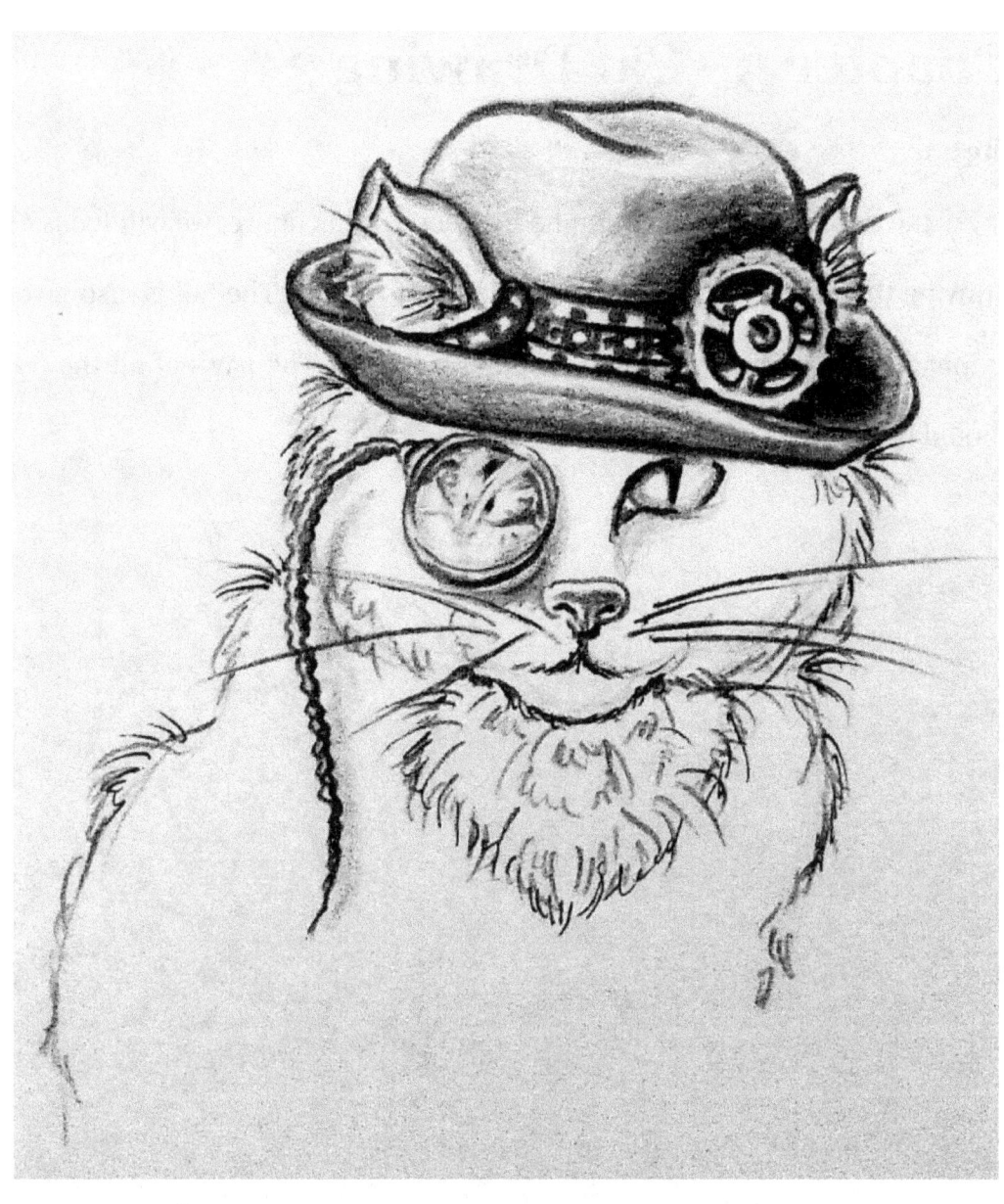

Chapter 3 - Cat Drawing 3

Step 1

Draw the outline of a cat bent on its forefeet. In this figure, we will focus on drawing the machine parts inside the body of the cat. The tail is also given emphasis and hence drawn in a long curved form. The paws of all the feet should be drawn carefully.

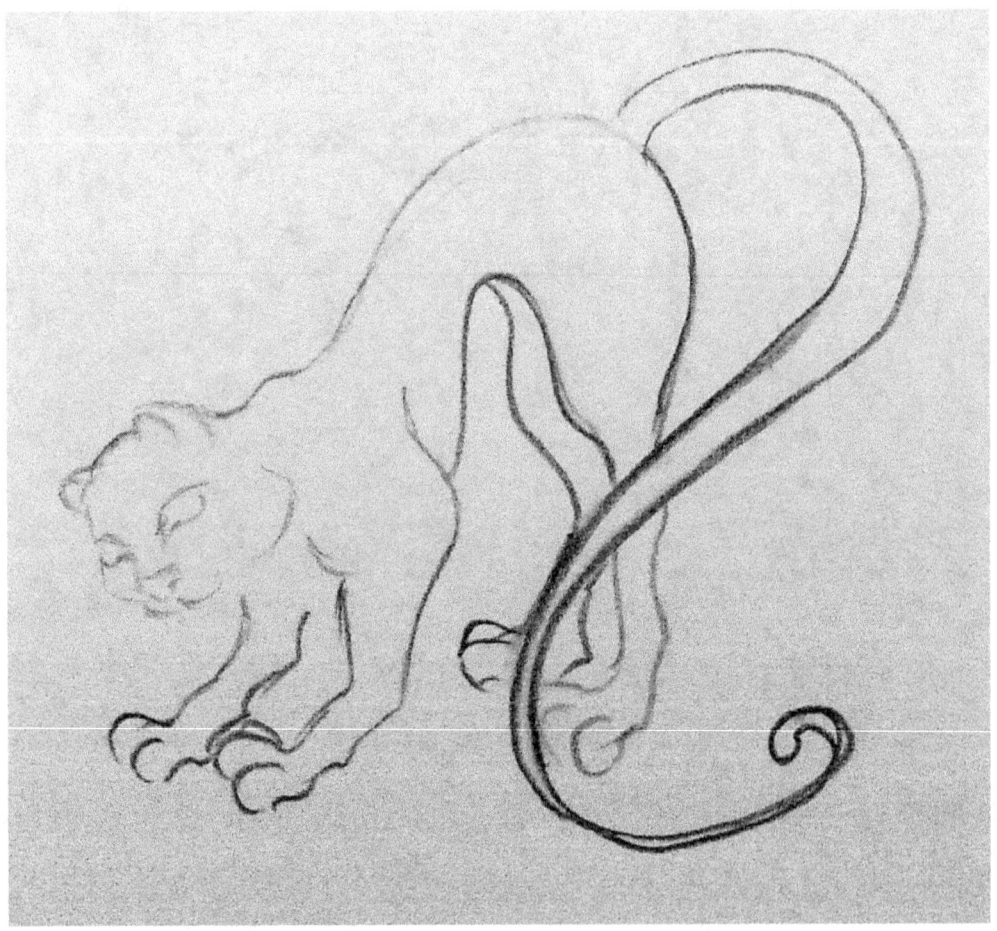

Step 2

Draw the outline of the face, eyes, ears, nose and mouth of the cat. Draw the bands on the forefeet. There are strips of fasteners on both the edges of these bands. Give a little shading in the bands.

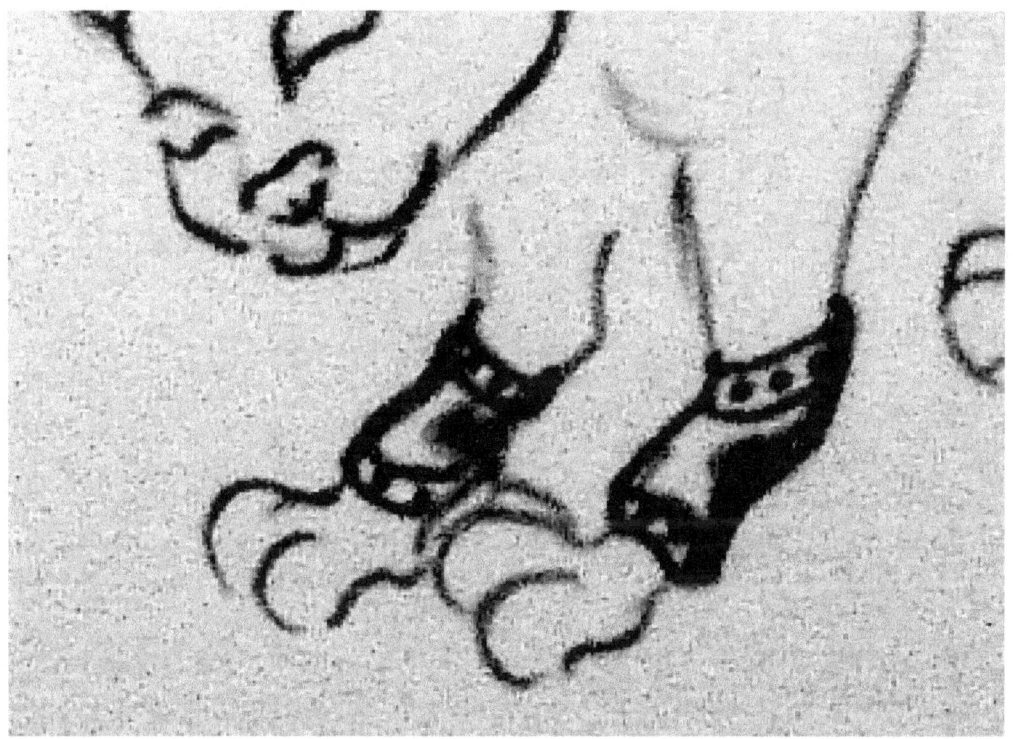

Step 3

In this step, we will create some hollow spaces in the body of the cat so that we can insert some machine parts inside. Draw the outline of these hollow areas. One such portion is drawn in the face and the other is drawn in the frontal body. You can also draw a hint of gears and fasteners inside the hollow areas.

Draw the details of the eyes, nose and mouth as well. In this illustration, we will not give much focus on the features of the face because the body is given more emphasis.

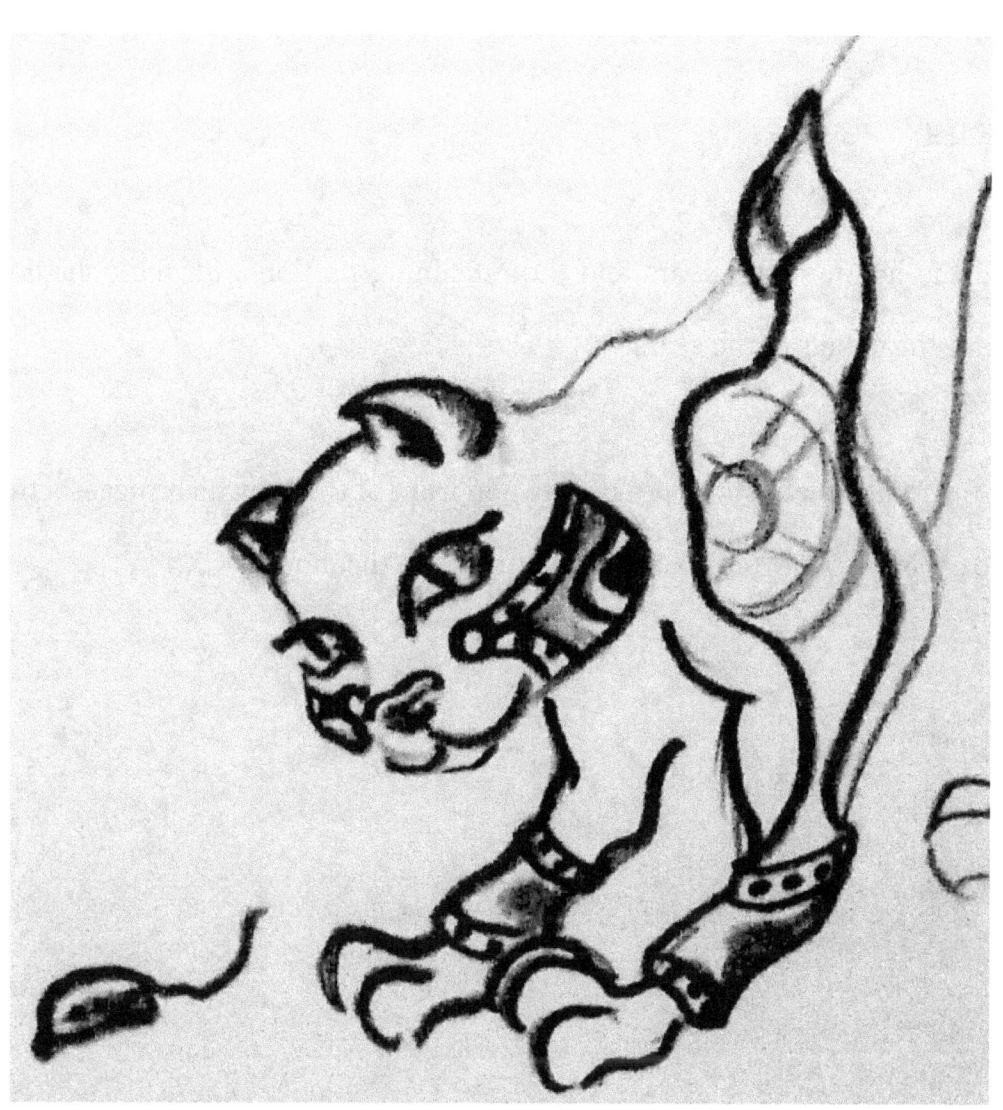

Step 4

Fill the hollows with gears and the remaining portion with dark shading. Draw the details of the gears.

A figure like that of a mouse is drawn in front of the cat which suggests that the cat is probably programmed to hunt down the mouse.

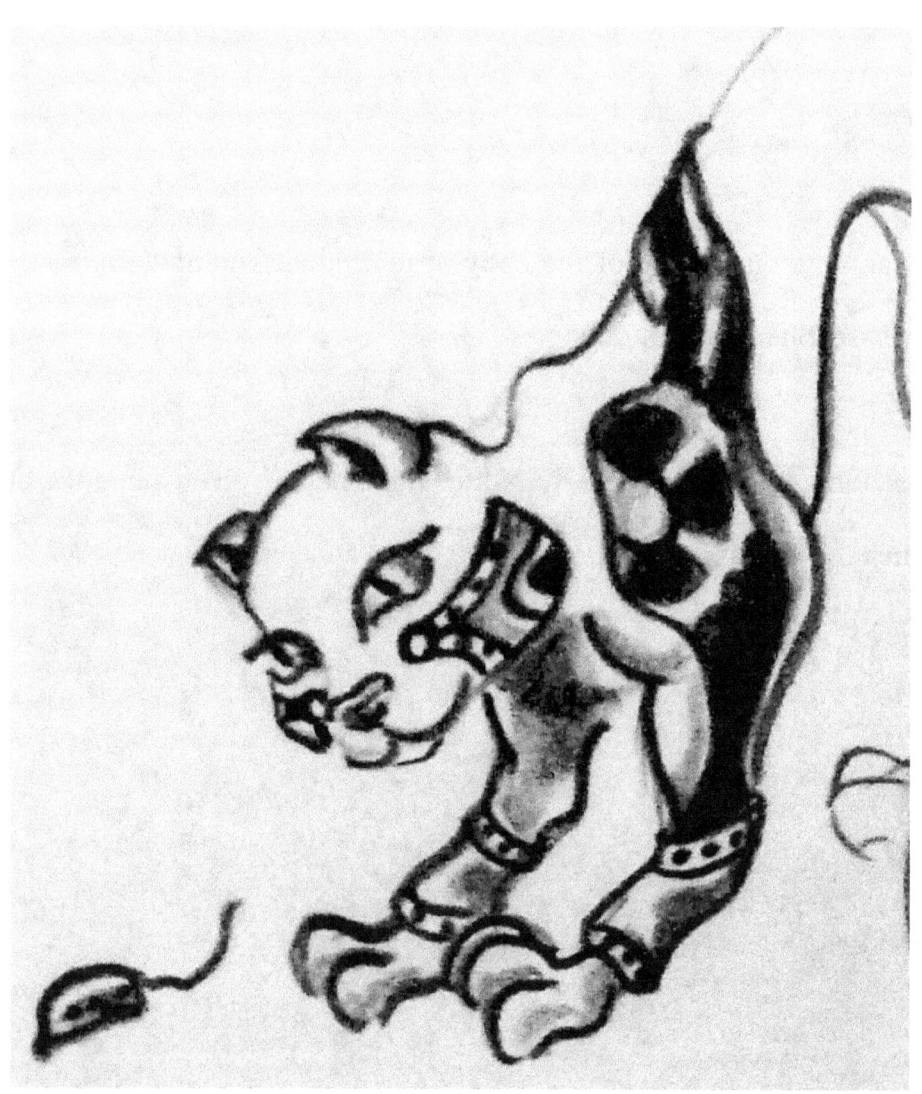

Step 5

Draw an antenna on top of the body of the feline. The antenna rests on a

heavy base. Shade the antenna.

Give shading to the frontal body. Notice the stitching given along the hollow

in which the gear is inserted.

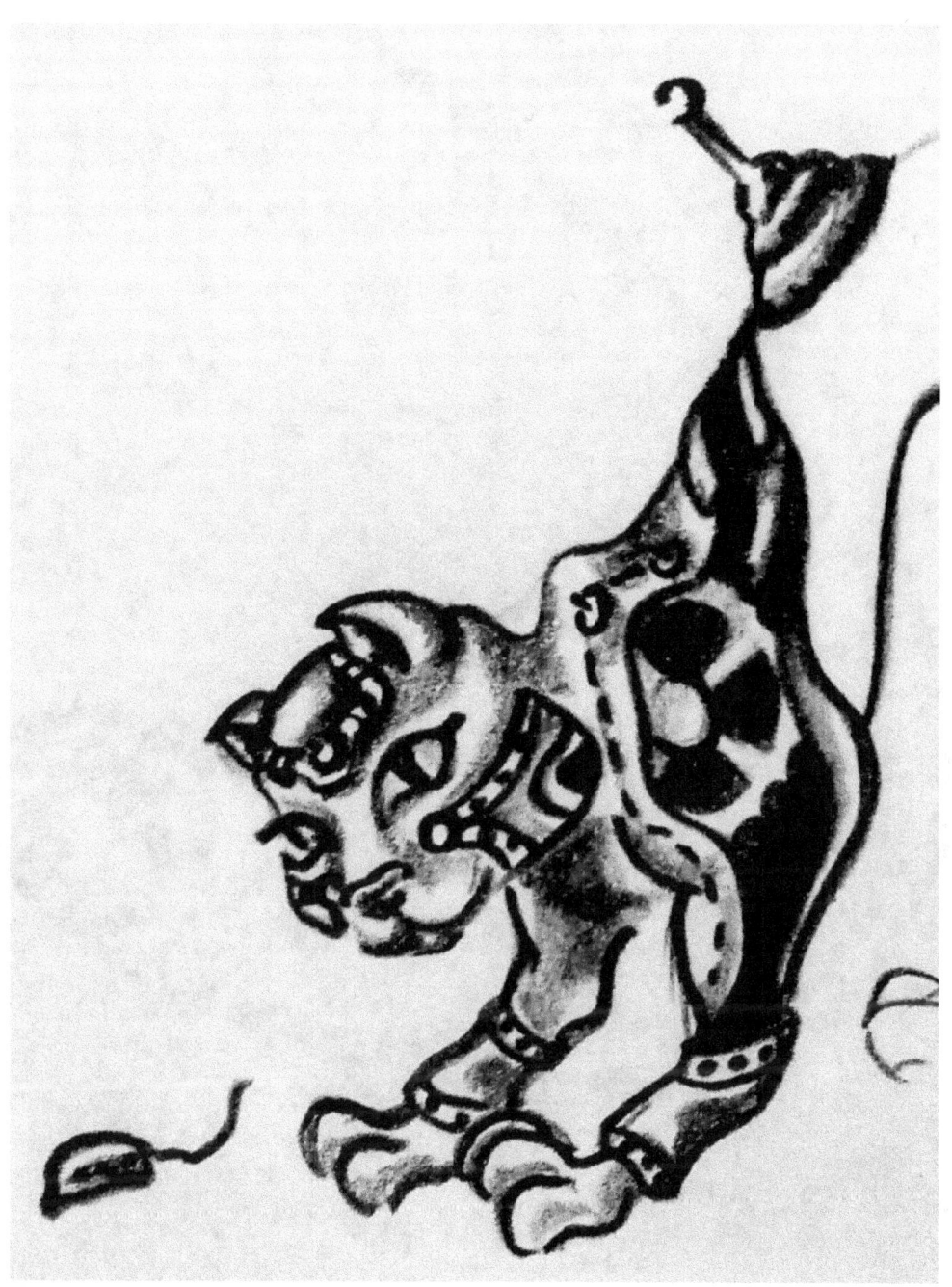

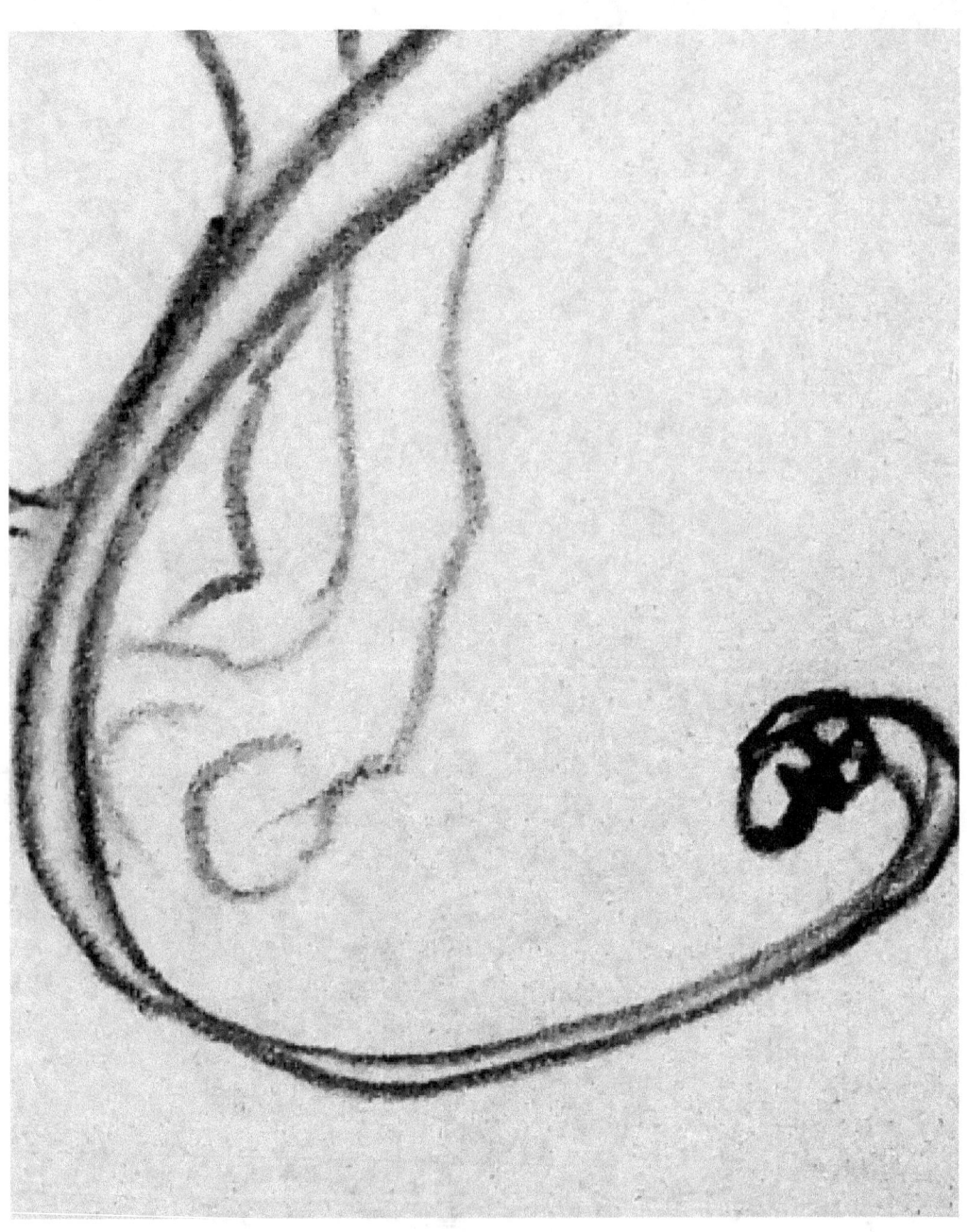

Step 6

Draw a long stitching along the back edge of the hollow portion.

Give shading to the hind portion of the body. The hind legs are drawn adjacent to each other. Thus, the partially visible leg is given darker shading.

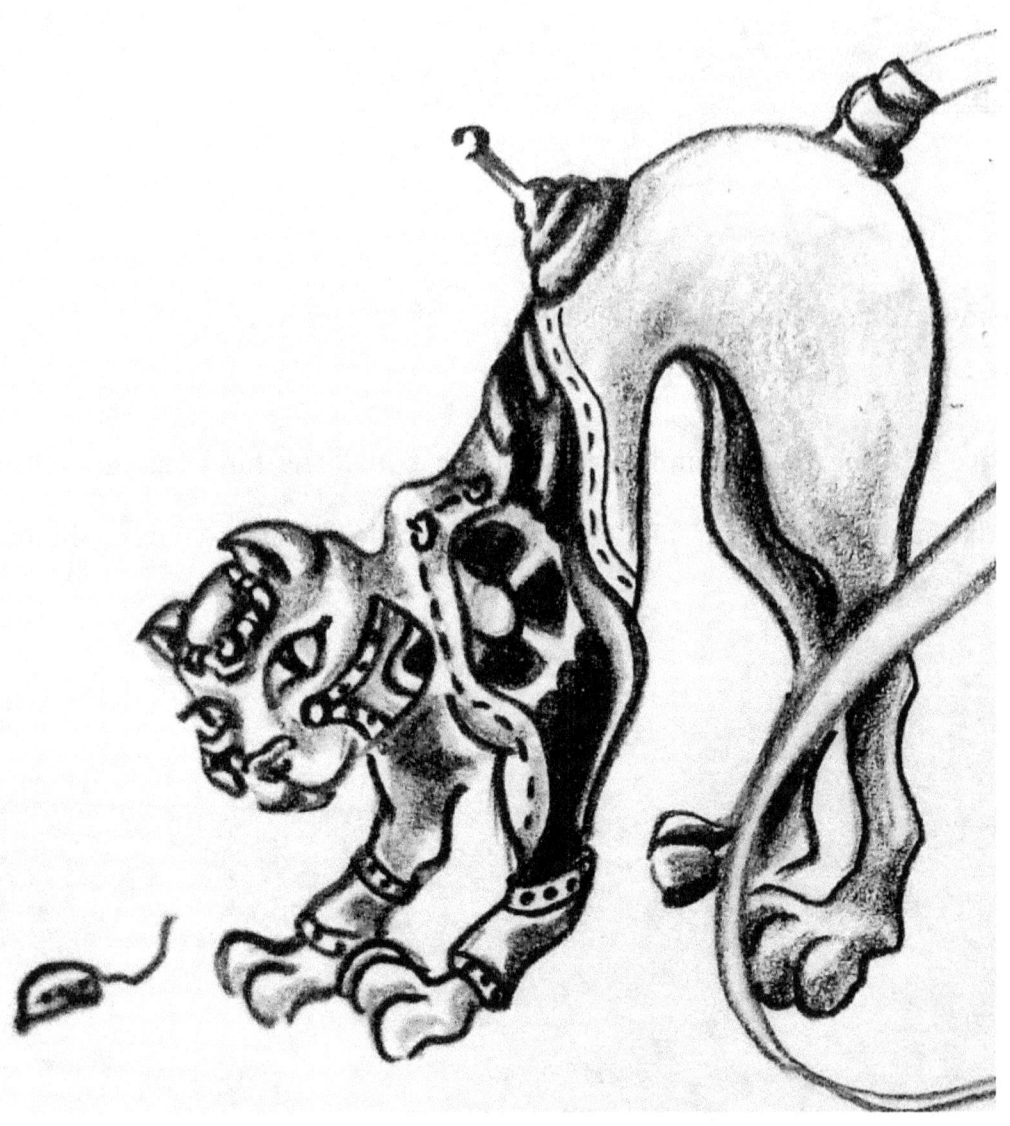

Step 7

Draw a band where the tail of the cat is beginning. Give shading in the tail. The end of the tail also consists of a rattle like that of a rattle snake. This gives a suggestion of a powerful tail of the cat which is used to can kill its prey.

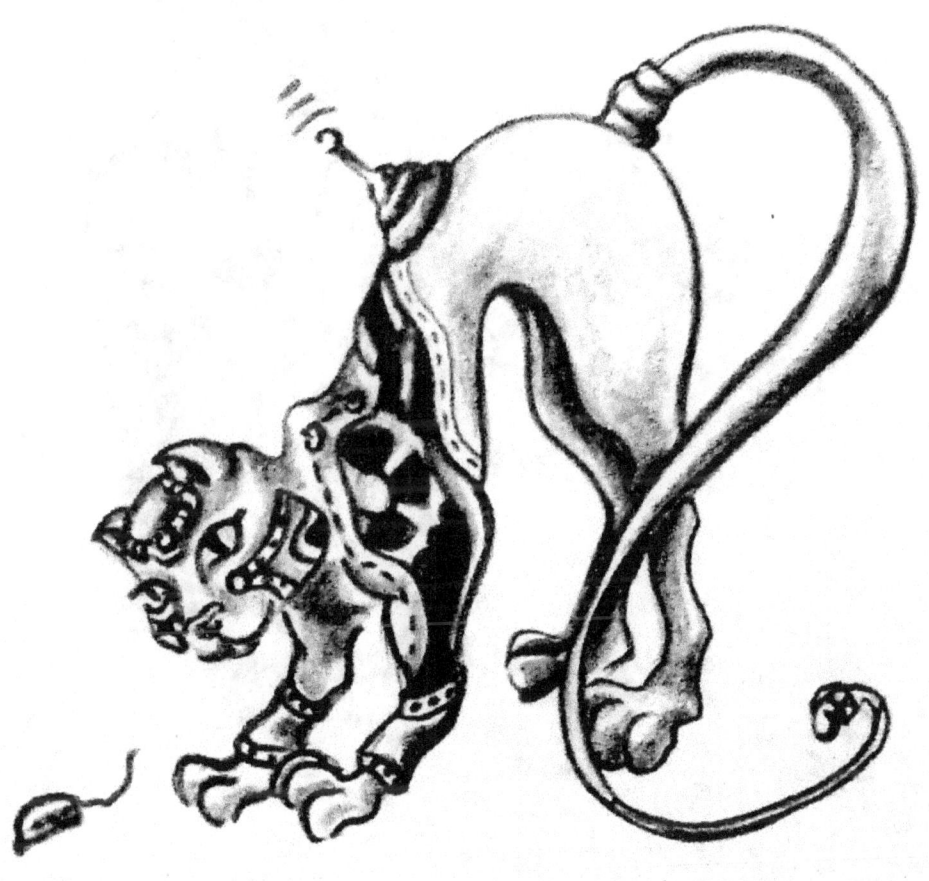

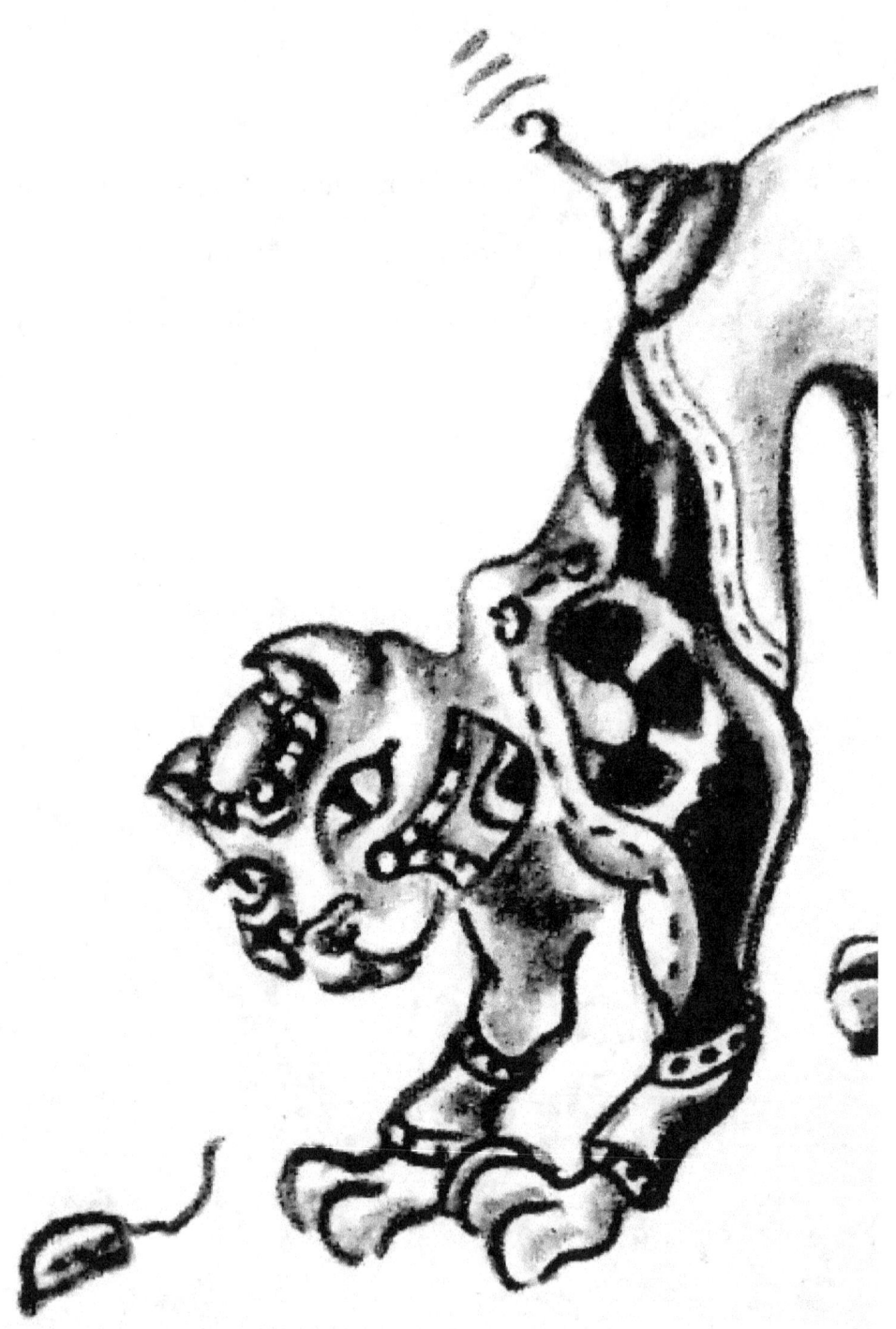

Step 8

Complete the Steampunk cat by giving finishing touches to the illustration.

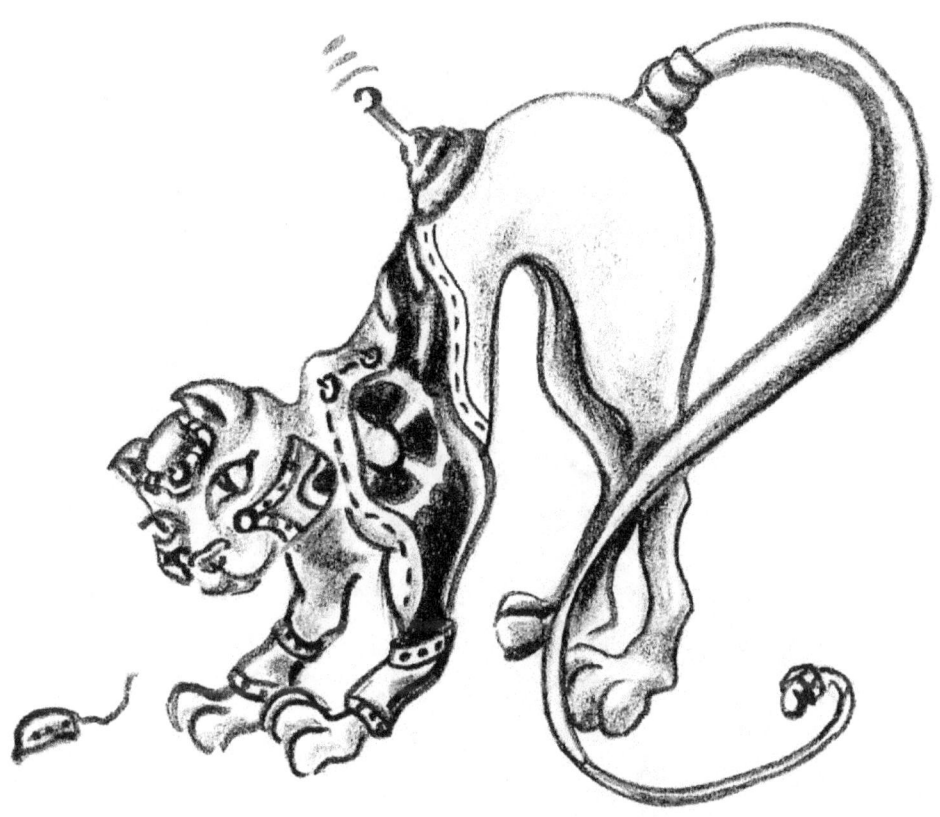

Chapter 4 - Cat Drawing 4

Step 1

We will draw a non-living cat in the form of a toy in this illustration. Draw the outline of the cat. The feline is portrayed as sitting in a baby cot.

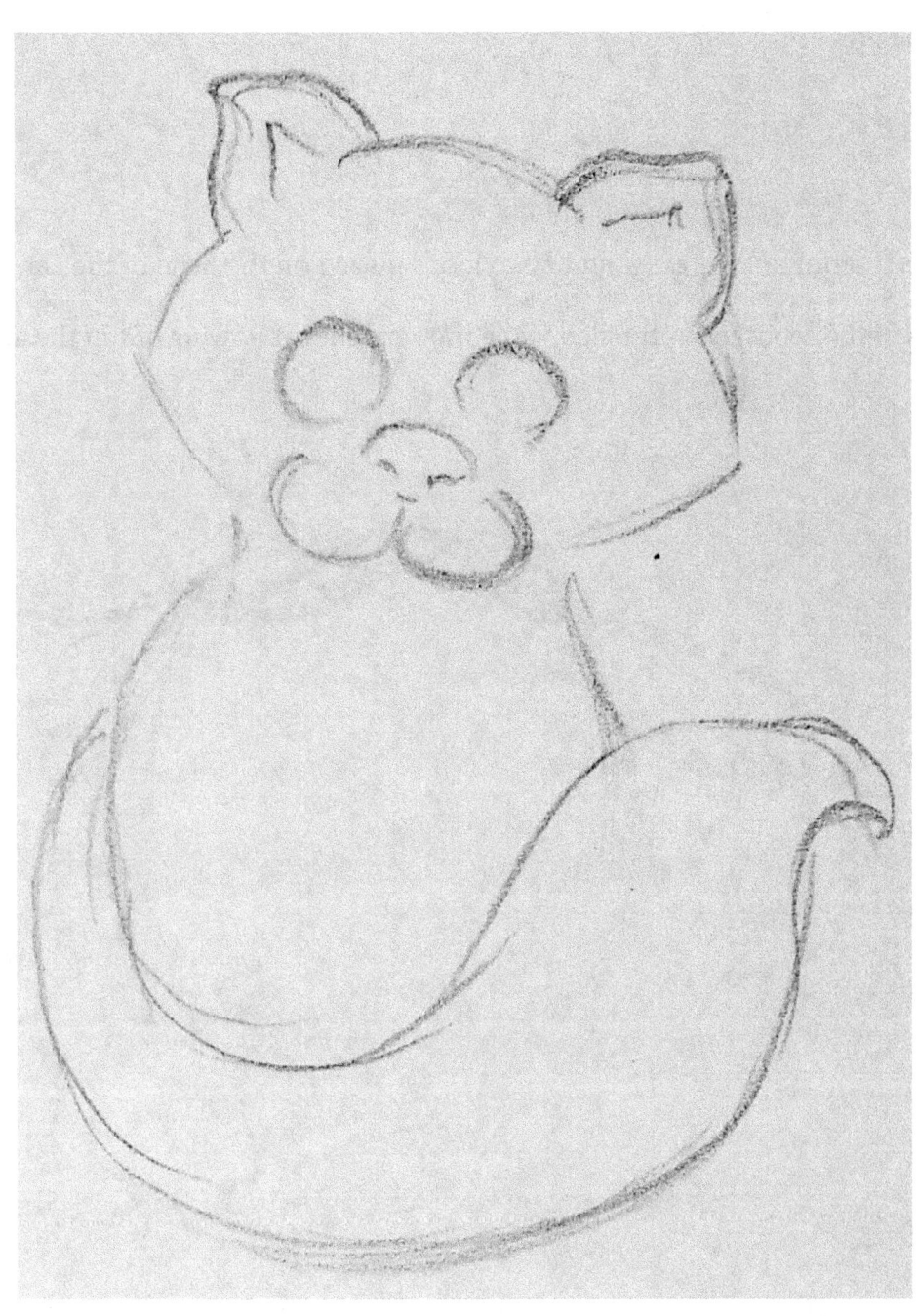

Step 2

Draw a scourge emerging out of two loops placed on the head of the cat. The ends of the scourge are tangled while they are shown flowing out in the air.

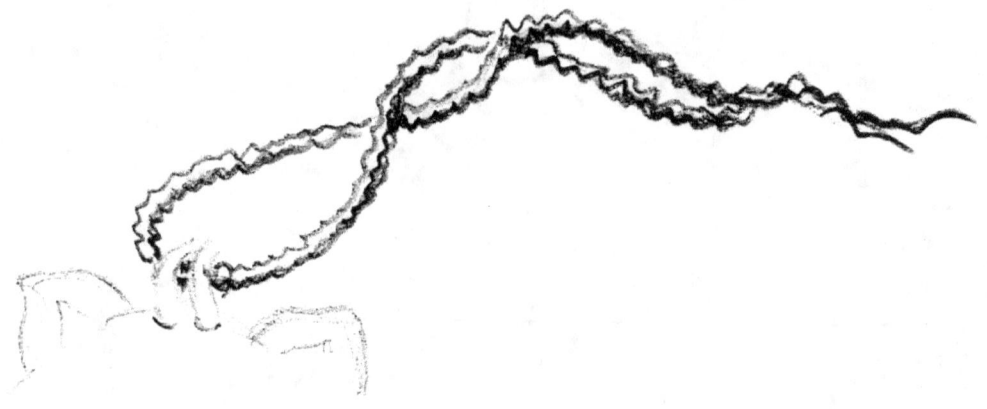

Step 3

Draw the loops on the head from which the scourge is emerging out. Draw a piece of metal placed on left eye of the cat.

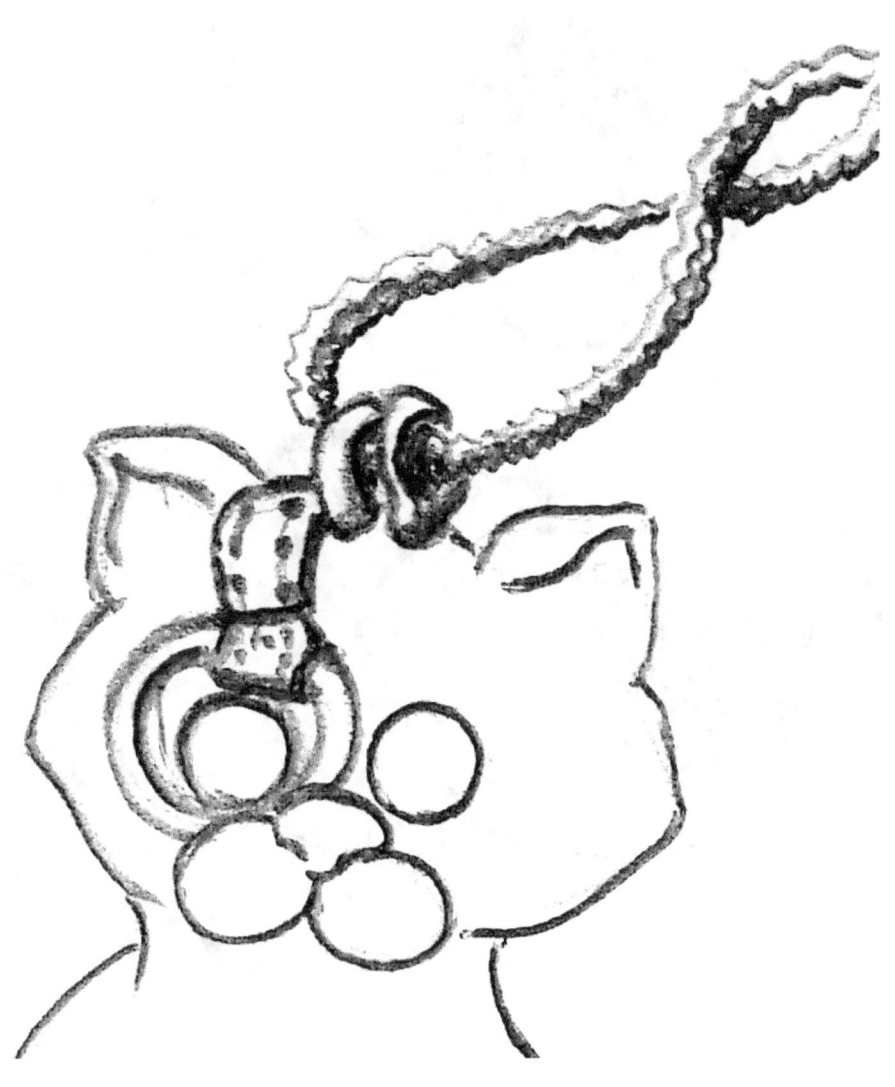

Step 4

Draw a gear on the body. Notice the "+" sign on this gear. The other machine part on the right side of the body is drawn in the shape of a bean. A belt is also encompassing this bean shaped part of machinery.

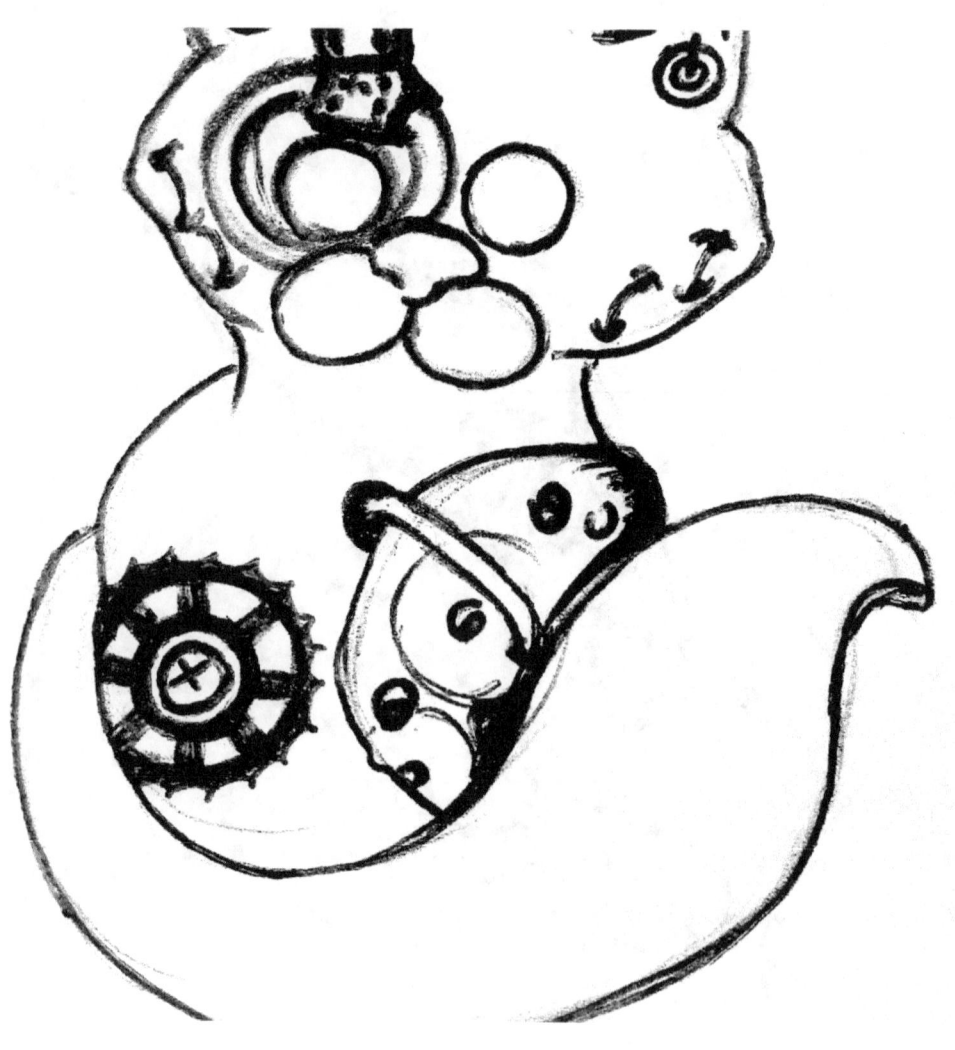

Step 5

The cot, in which the cat is sitting, is given a few drawings of a gear and another part resembling a metal sheet attached with some fasteners.

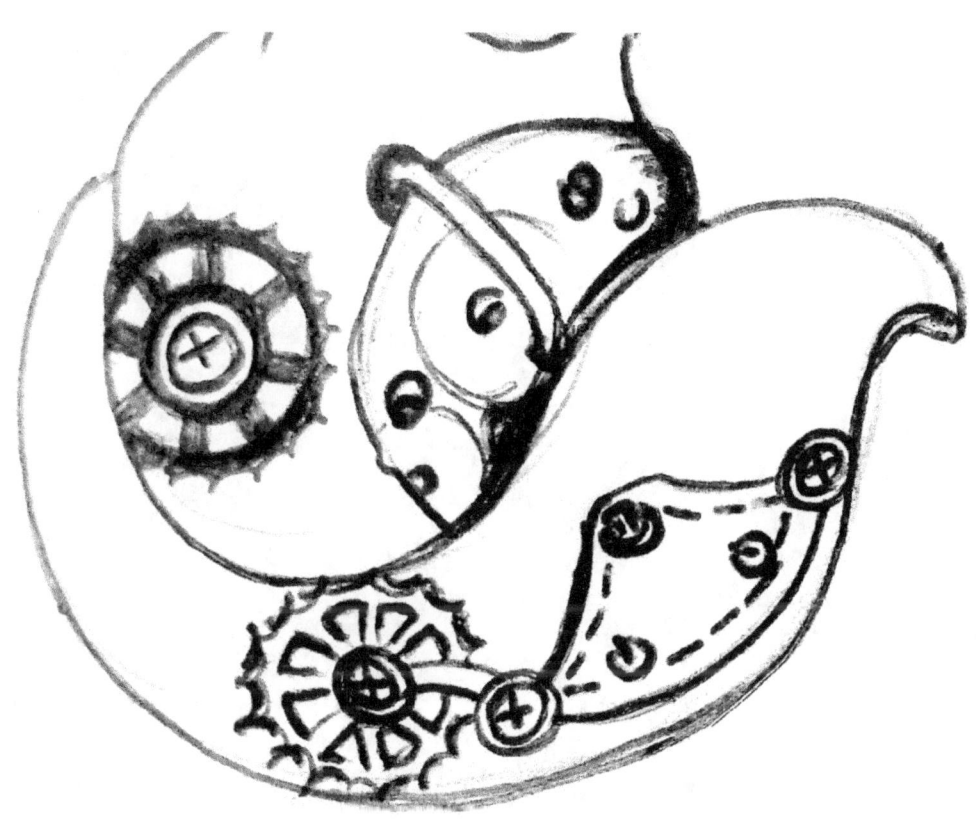

Step 6

Give some shading on the face of the cat. The eyes are given final shading and the mouth is also drawn in a different way. There are some stitches drawn on both sides of the face. Give slight shading in the neck as well.

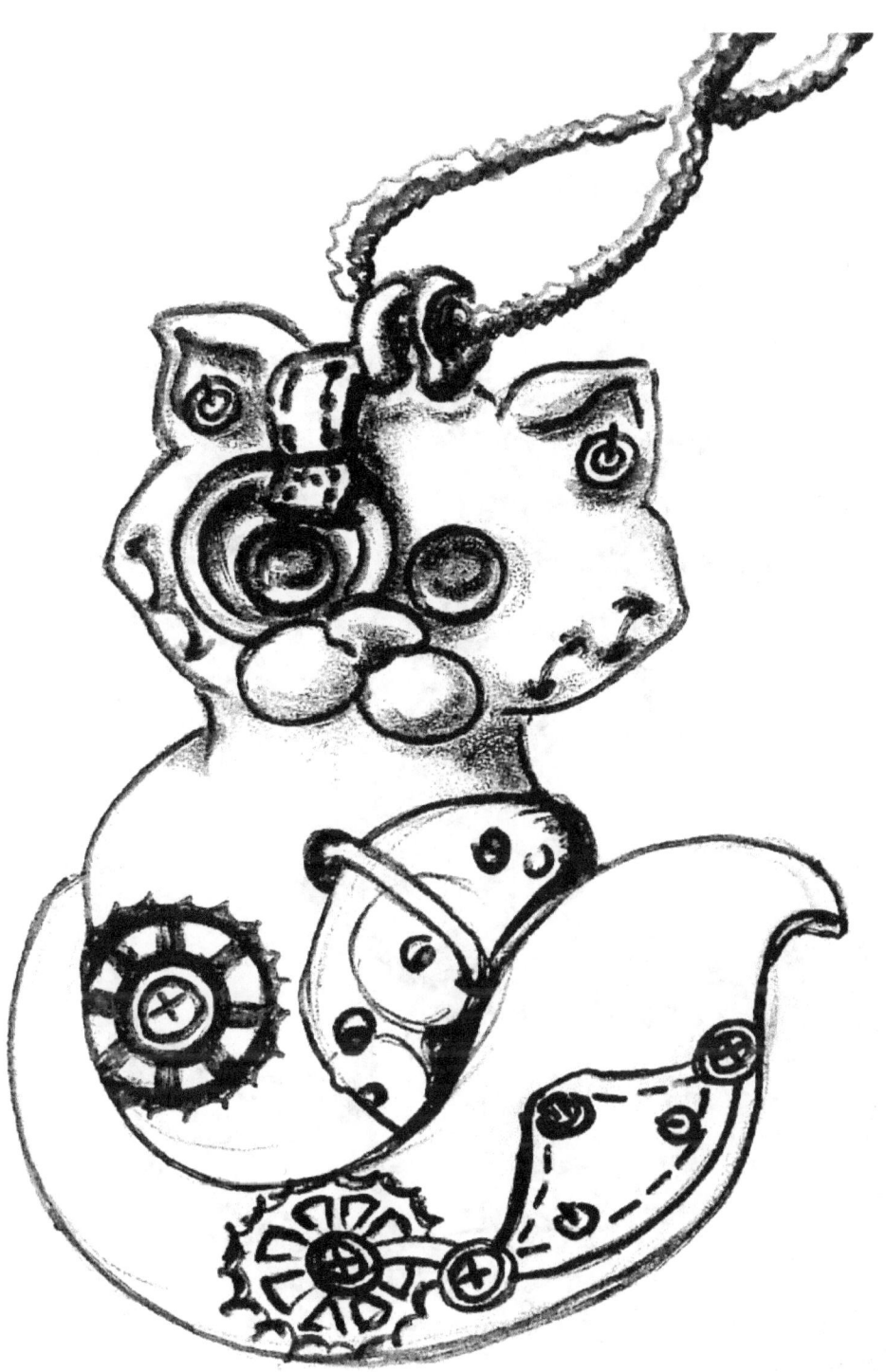

Step 7

Give shading in the rest of the body. The differences in gradation of shading make the toy cat lively.

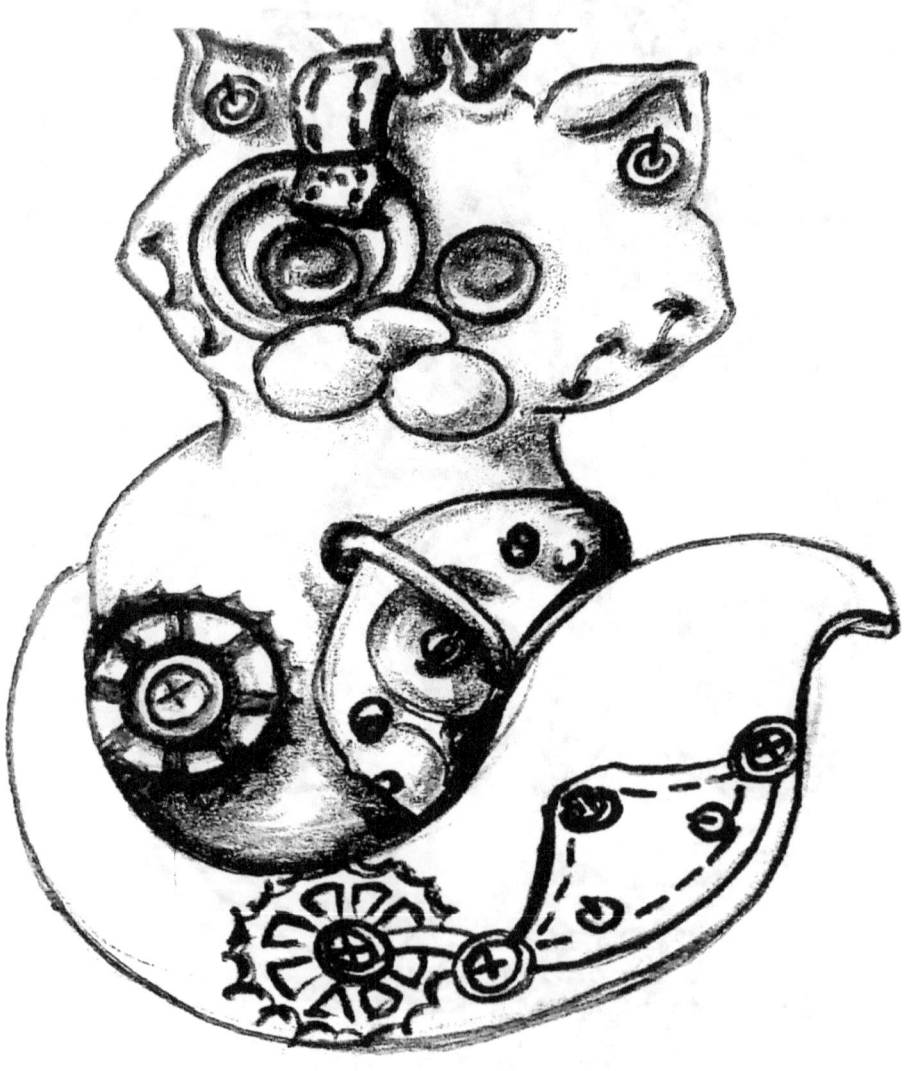

Step 8

Shade the toy cot of the feline and surround the machine parts with darker gradations of shading.

Give finishing touches to the illustration to complete the Steampunk toy cat.

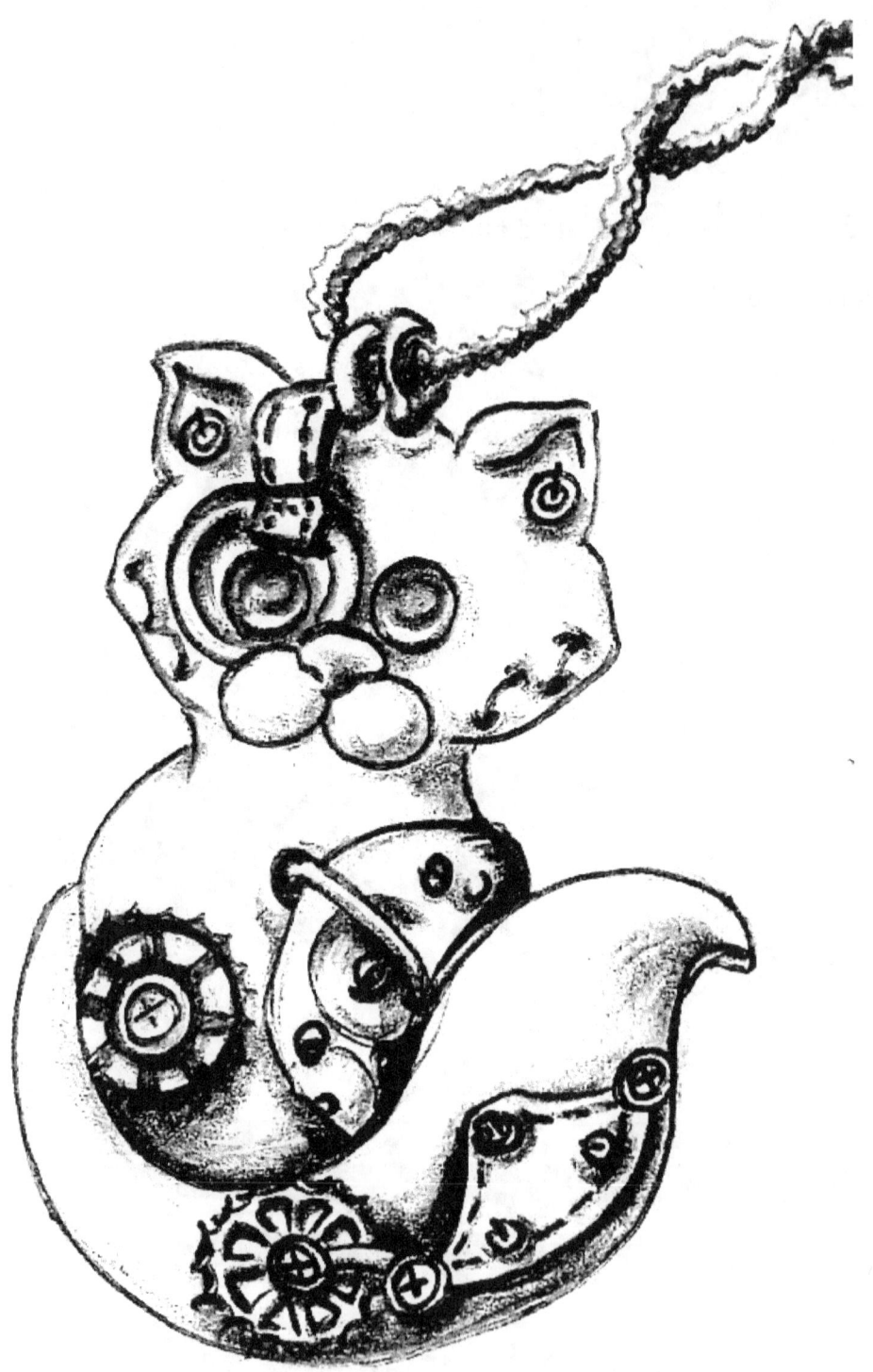

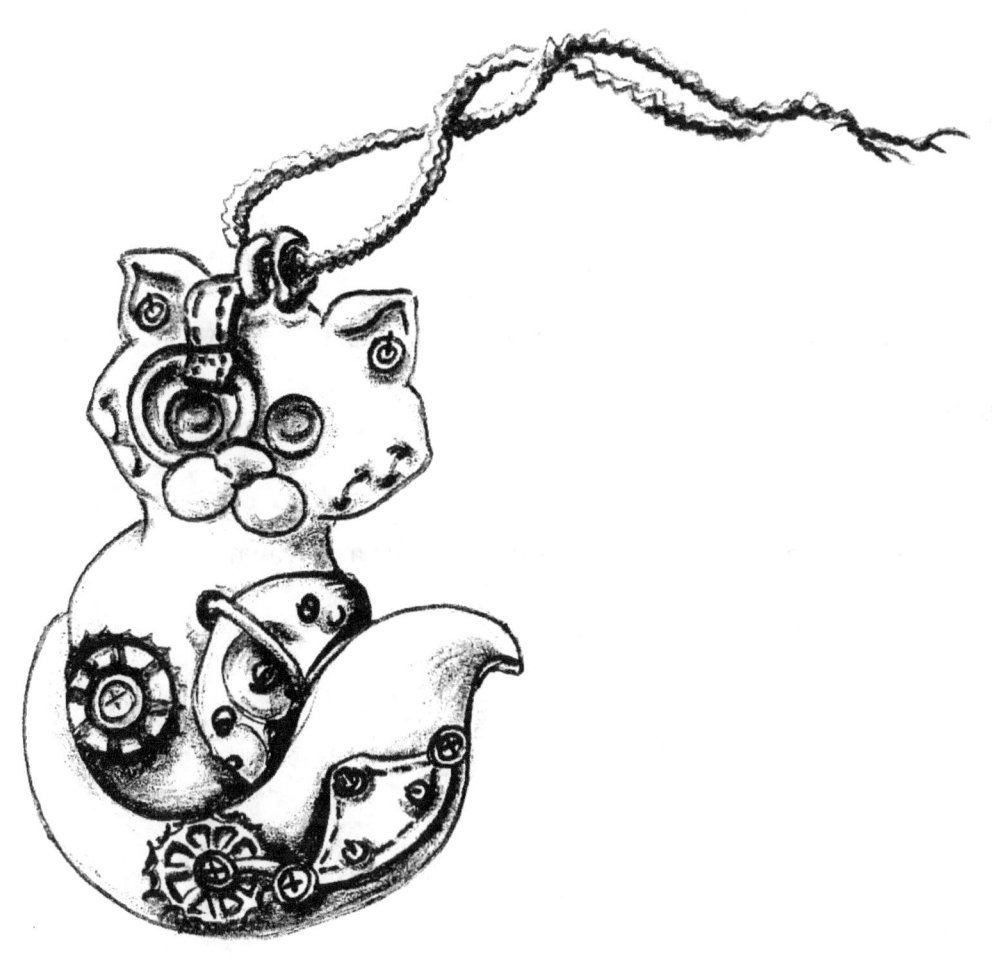

Chapter 5 - Cat Drawing 5

Step 1

Here, we are going to draw a cat which is wearing swimming goggles on its eyes. Thus, you do not have to make much effort to draw the eyes of this feline.

Draw the outline of the face. The body and face are drawn with slight details in this sketch because they are the second object in focus after the goggles.

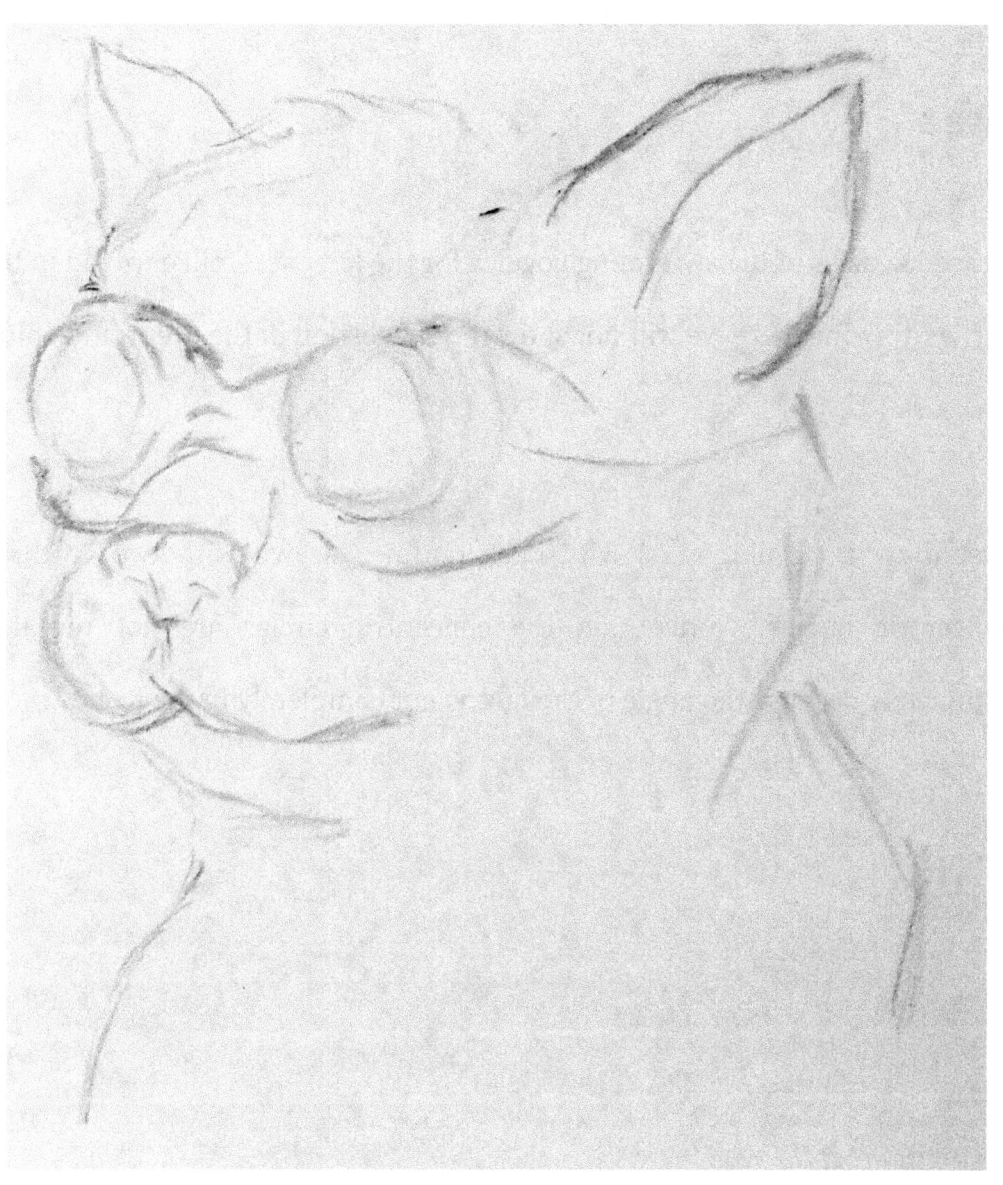

Step 2

Draw one glass of the swimming goggles for the left eye. Unlike we did in the earlier drawing, here we will not show the suggestion of the eye from behind the glass.

Just draw a circular glass with dark outlines drawn with two to three concentric circles. Notice that the concentric circles are not revealed completely because the angle of the face is not completely in the front.

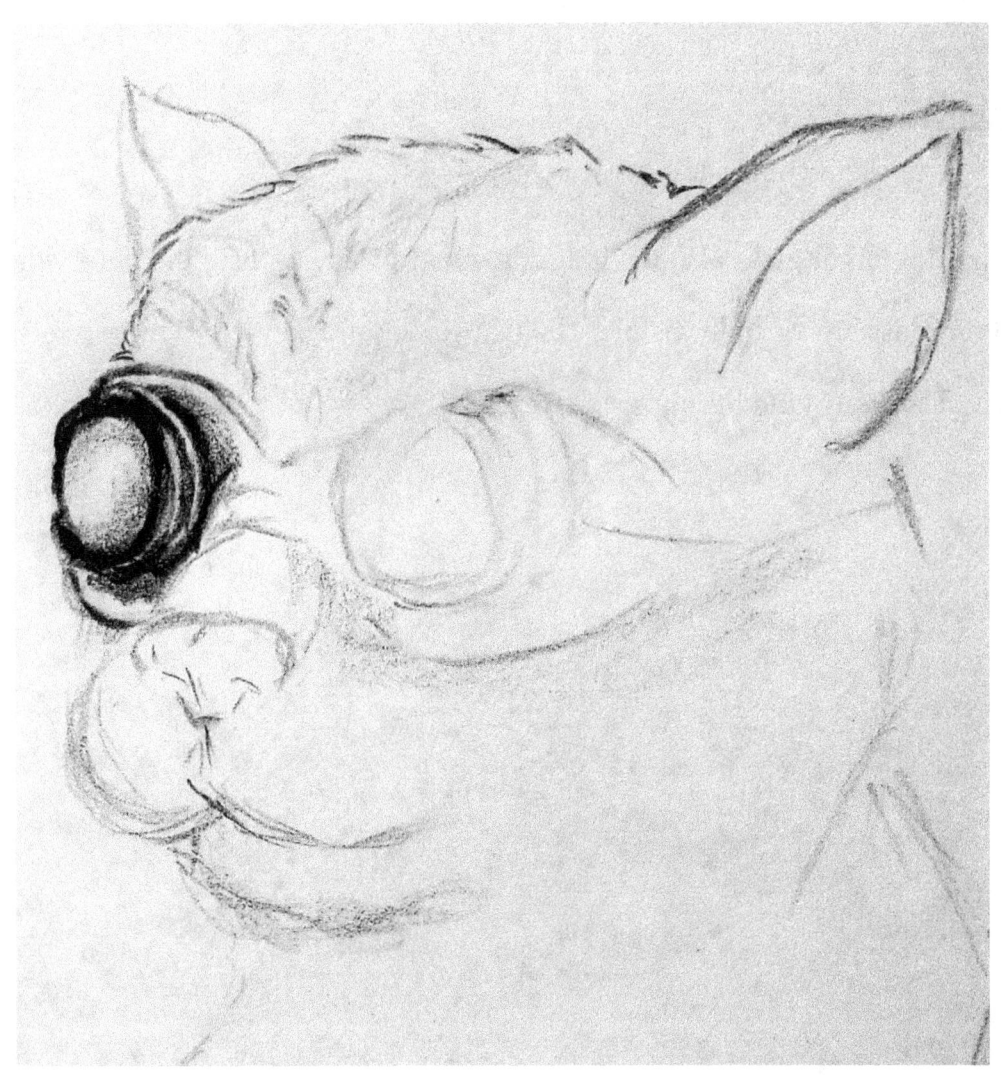

Step 3

Draw the other glass also for the right eye. In this eye also, the outer edges of the glass are partially visible. The two glasses are connected by two sets of arcs, like some kind of rubber bands.

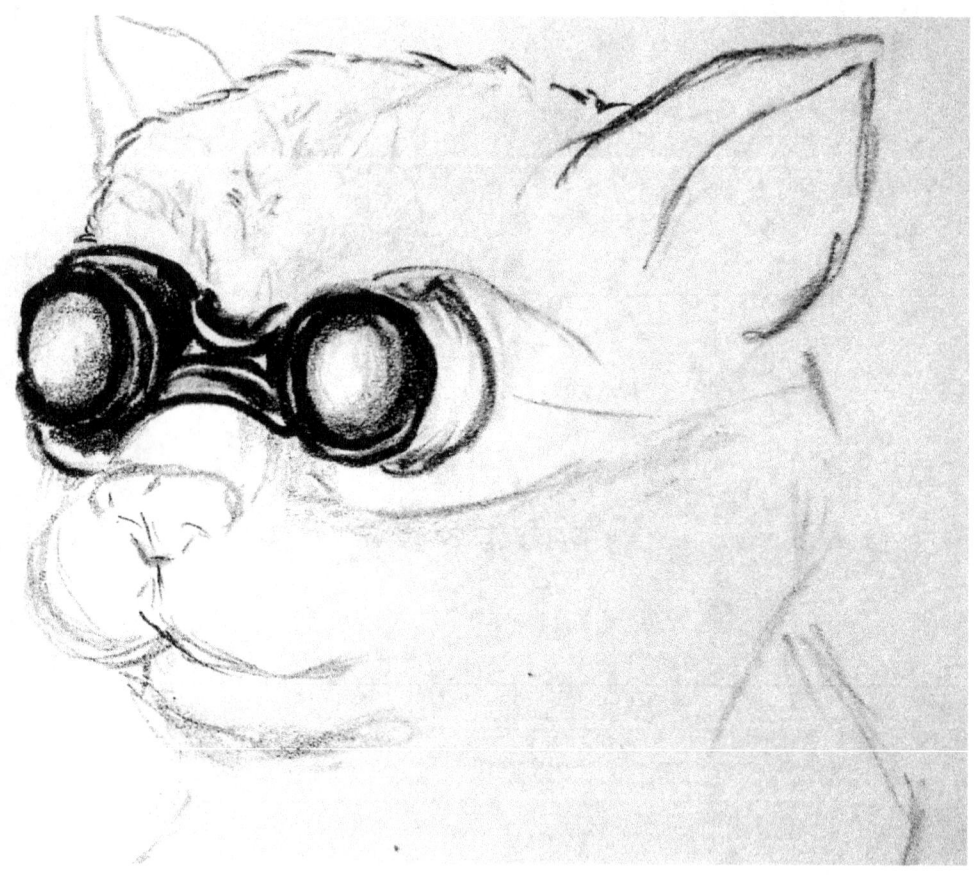

Step 4

In the end, these goggles are shown as connected with a wire to some other machine. Thus, here we will draw one circular component on the side of the right eye near the ear. You can draw it like a knob. You will figure out later what we are going to draw ultimately.

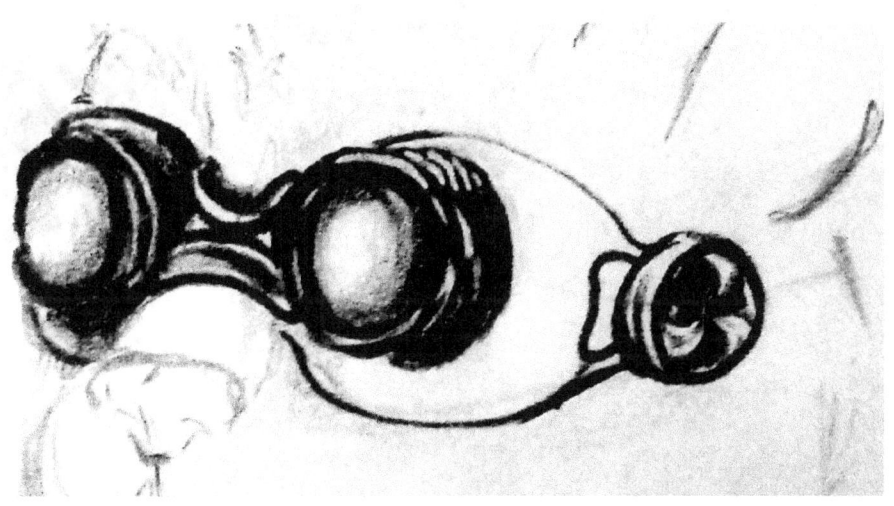

Step 5

Draw a circular dial around the right glass like that of the landline phones of Victorian era. Two fasteners are also drawn to attach the knob with the dial.

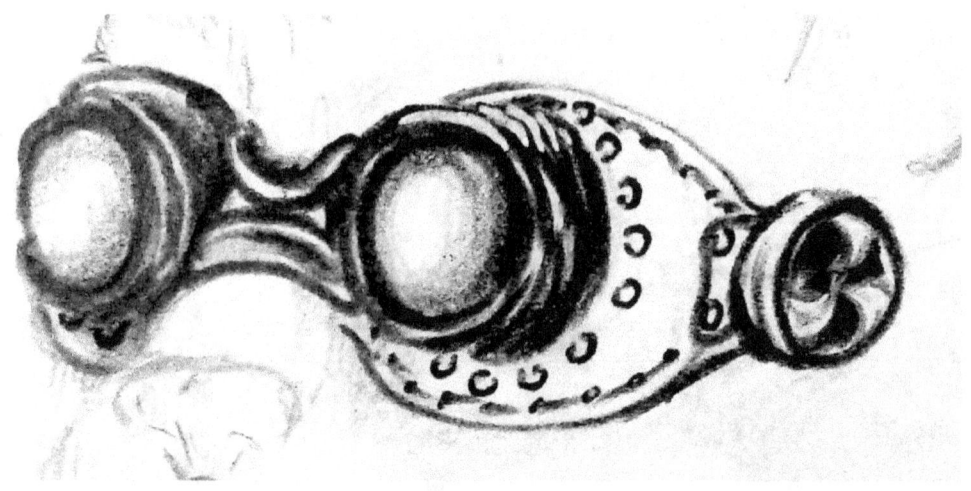

Step 6

Give shading to the dial. The numbers or the fasteners of the dial are enhanced by the darker shading around them.

Draw a spiral wire emerging from the knob and going behind the head.

Draw the outline of a gear near the neck connected to the knob with a kind of shaft. Another shaft is also coming out of this gear directed towards the right glass.

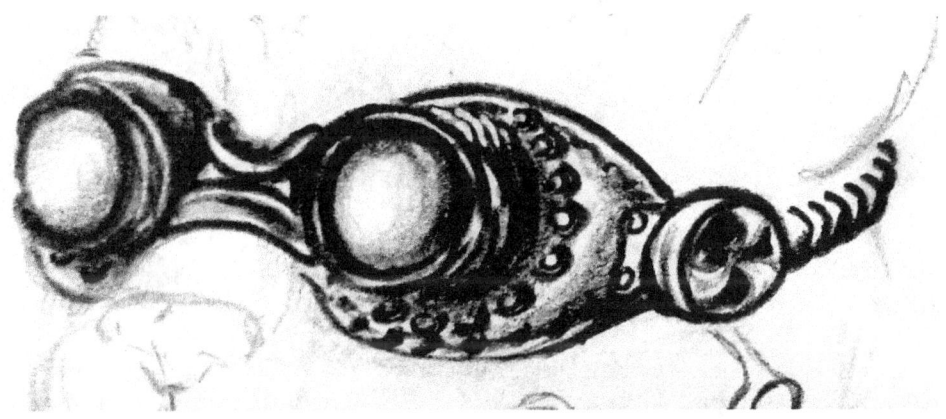

Step 7

Highlight the gear and its shafts with darkened outlines and shading inside them. The other shaft near the right glass is also given highlighting.

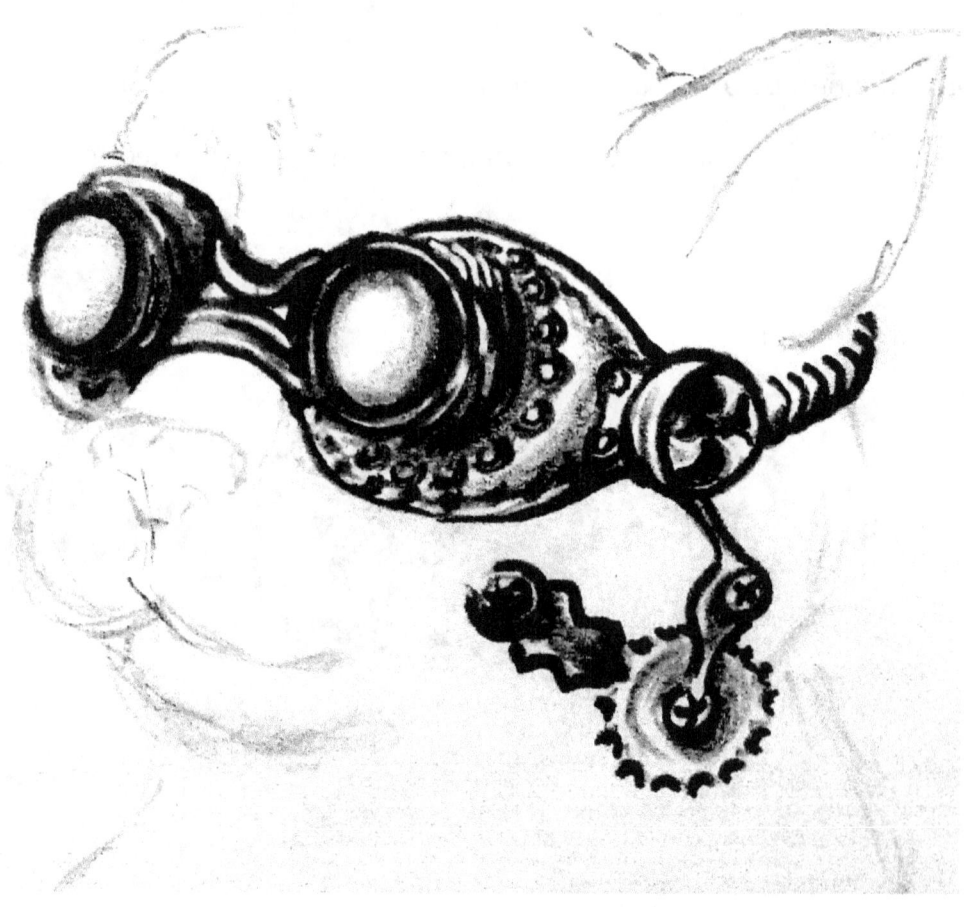

Step 8

Draw the furry details on the head and ears of the cat with small strokes of lines. Give slight shading as well.

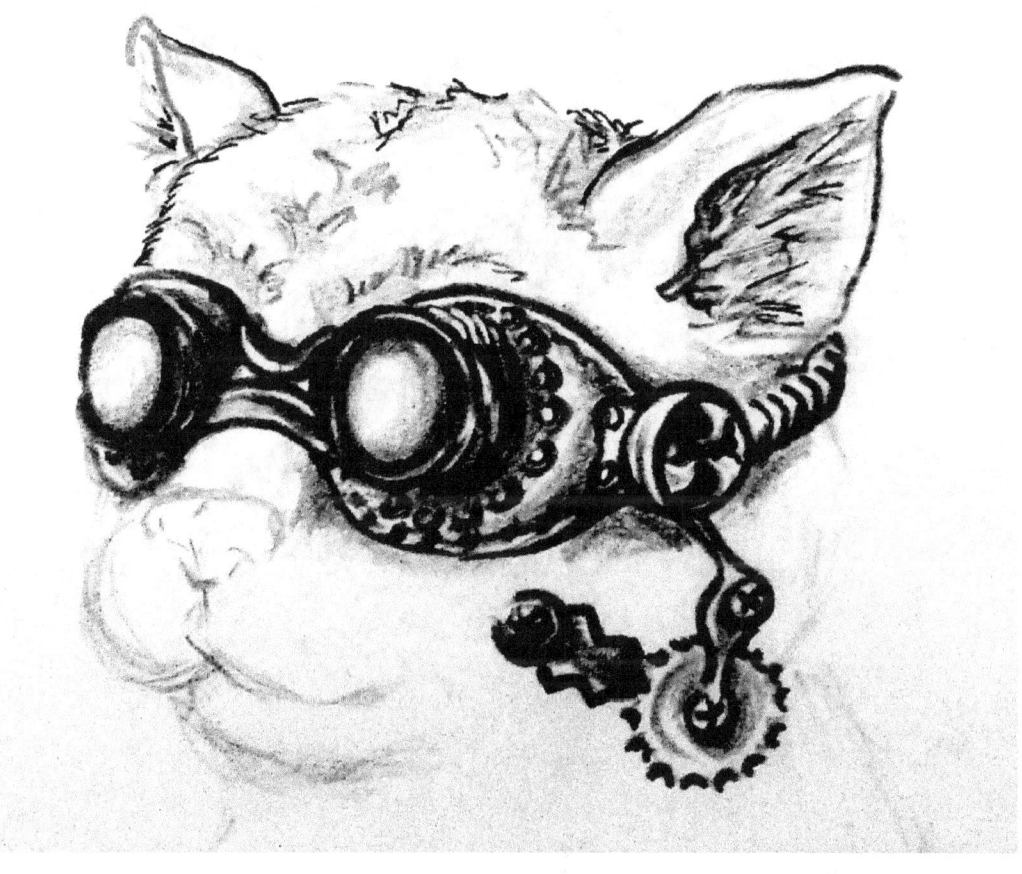

Step 9

Draw fur on the remaining face of the cat. Complete the nose with lines and shading. Give shading near the small gear and its shafts.

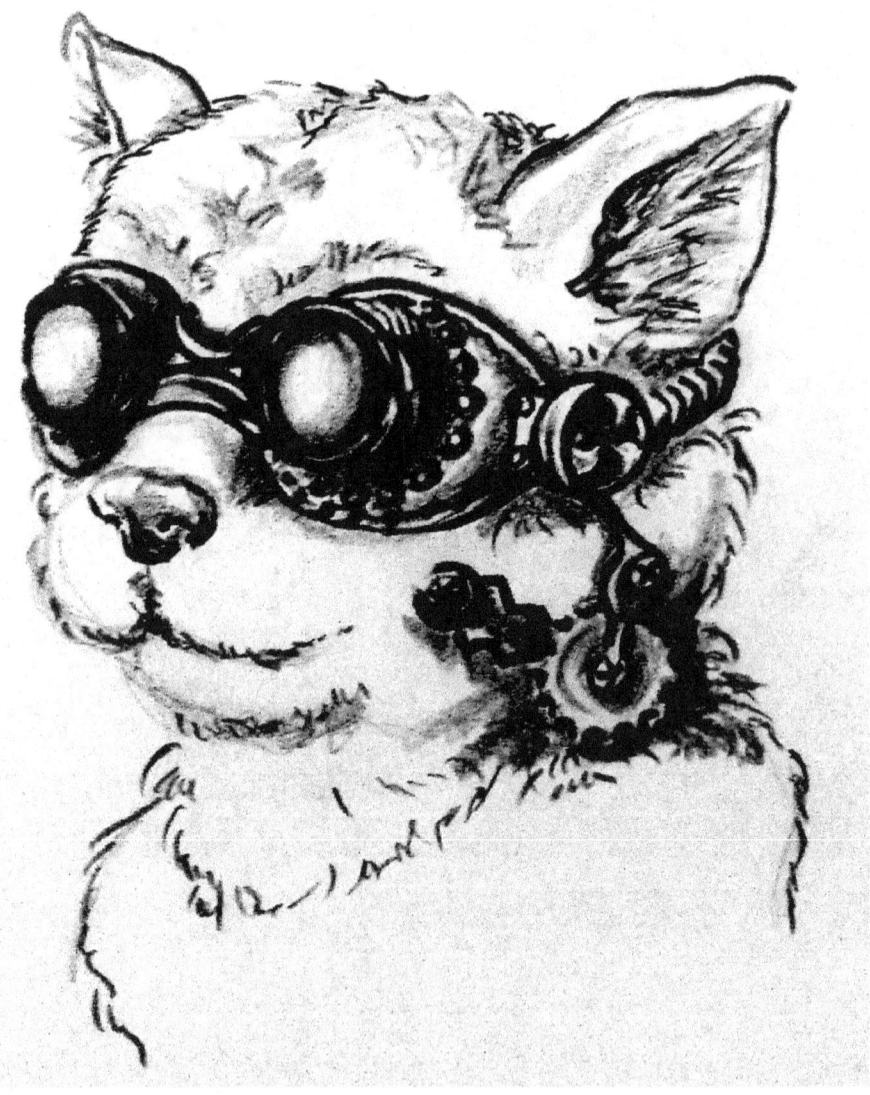

Step 10

Complete the drawing by shading the body of the cat. Give finishing touch to the shading of the glasses of swimming goggles. The centers of the glasses are given very light shading to give a suggestion of reflected light.

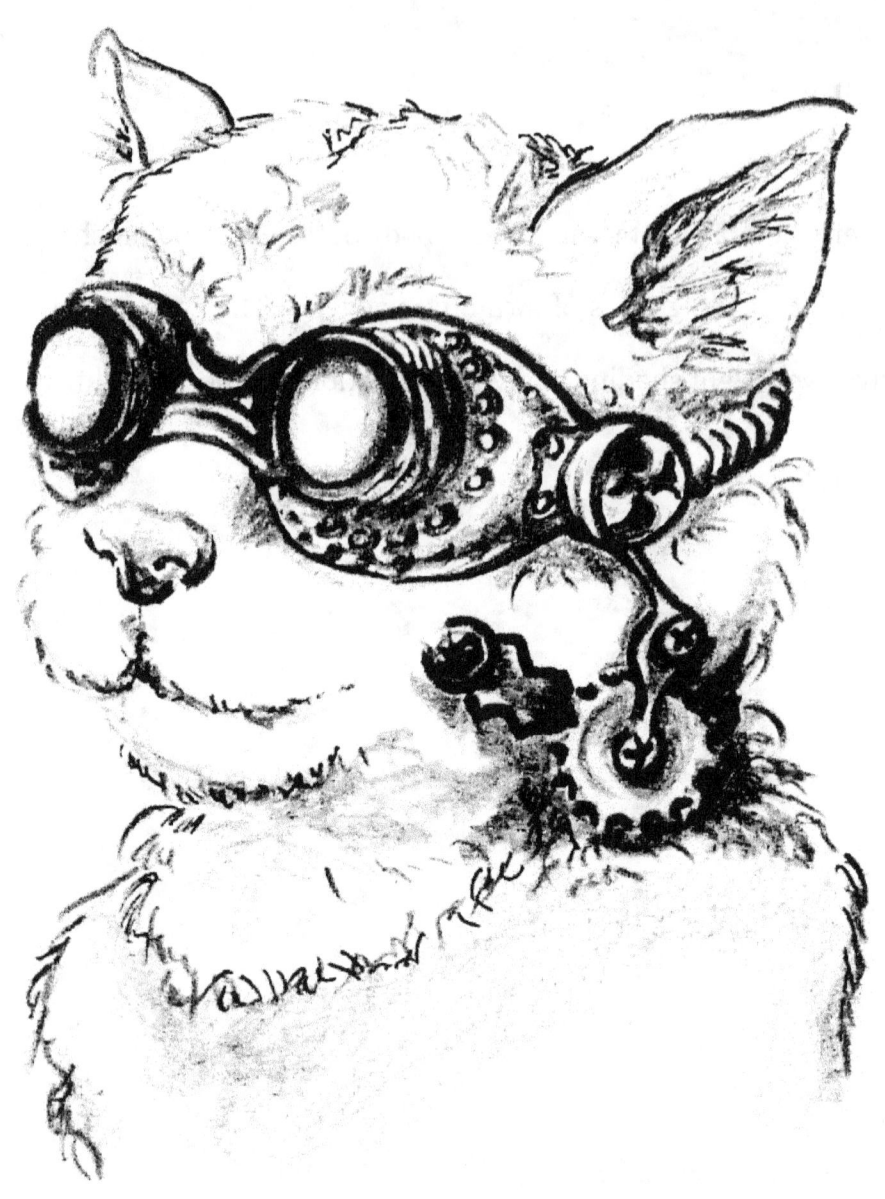

Chapter 6 - Cat Drawing 6

In this chapter, we are going to draw a robotic Steampunk cat. The way we did before, we will create some hollow spaces in this animal's body and insert machinery in it.

Step 1

Draw the outline for the face of cat. The cat we are going to draw is a seemingly wicked. Thus, while drawing the features of the face, you should take care to make them a little sharp.

Draw the ears protruding upwards. The fur on the sides of the face are also turned outwards.

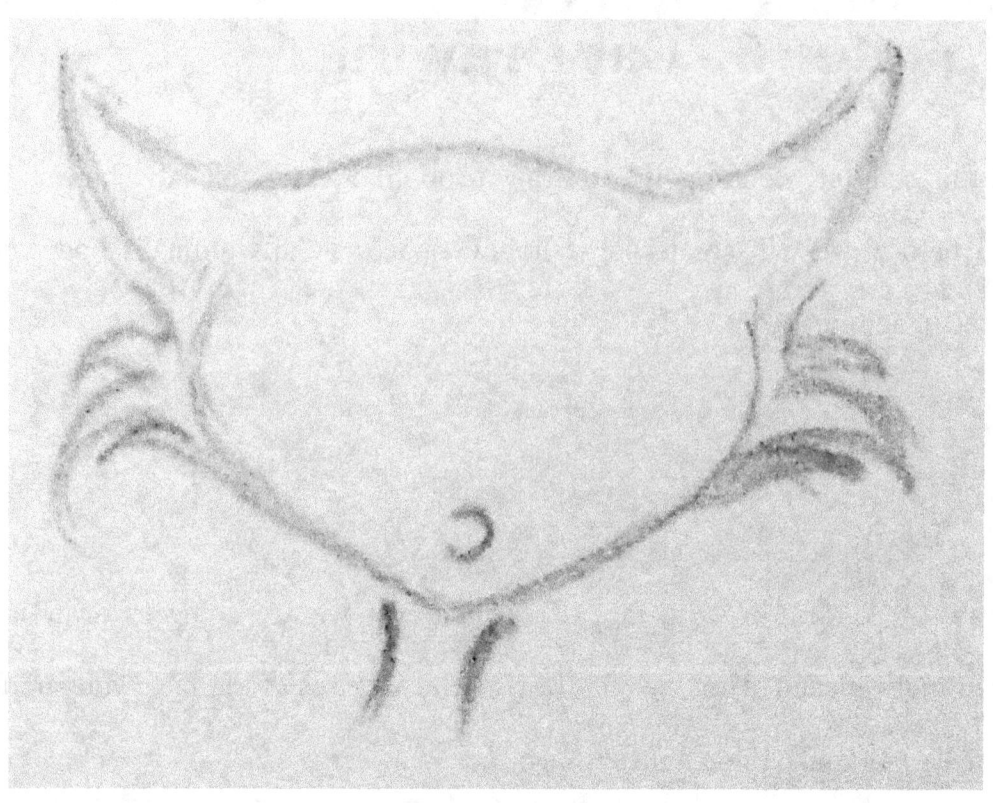

Step 2

Draw the outlines for the body and tail of the feline. The tail will be made as if it consists of several bony components, like that of a machine. At the tip of the tail, there is a knob like thing, which gives the feeling of a rattle.

You can also create the hollow shapes in the body, where we will insert the mechanical parts.

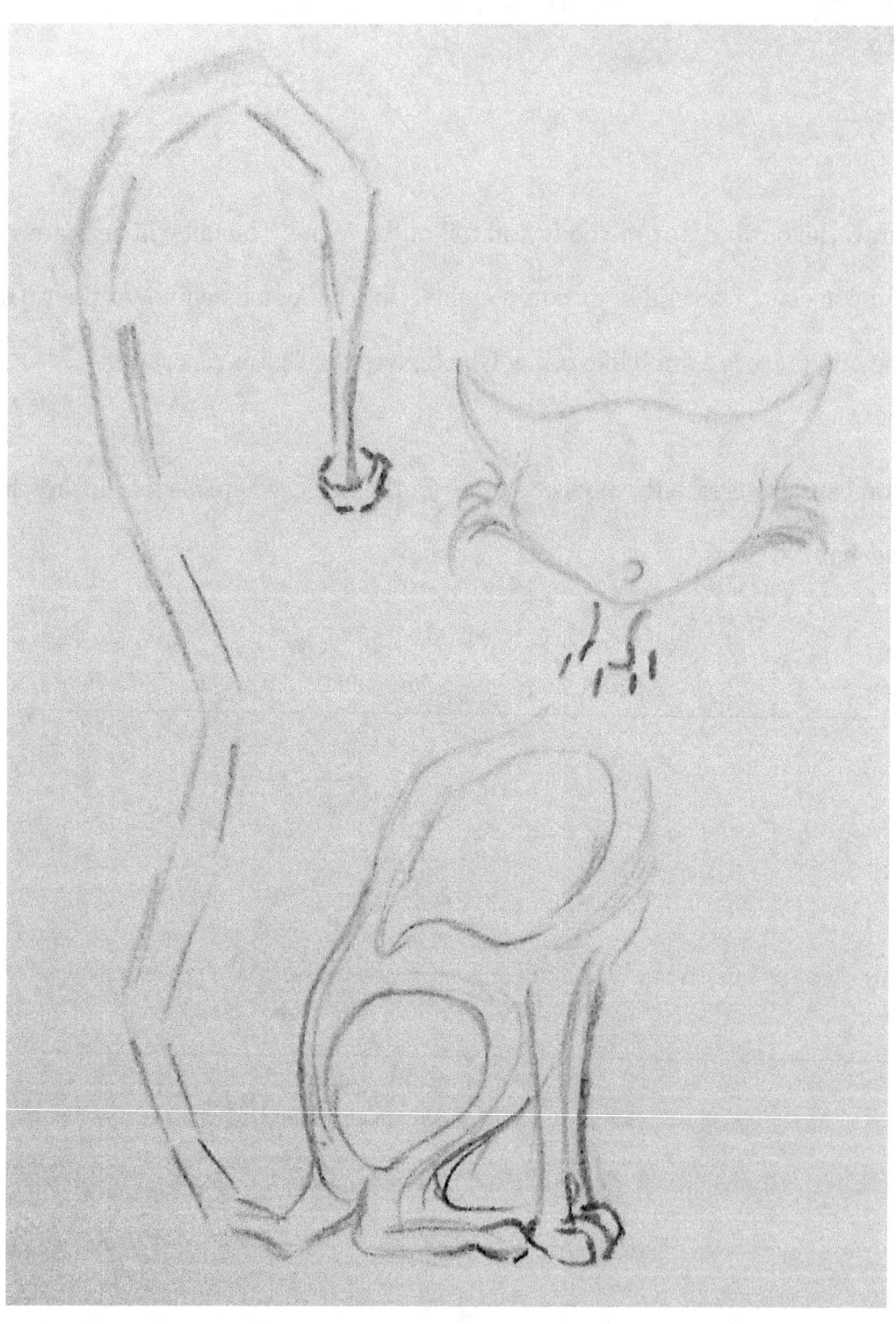

Step 3

Create a mask covering the eyes and forehead of the cat. The mask is also extending towards the ears. Draw the sharpened eyes as if they are of a wicked cat.

In the middle of the forehead, draw a gear. It seems like an embellishment on the forehead.

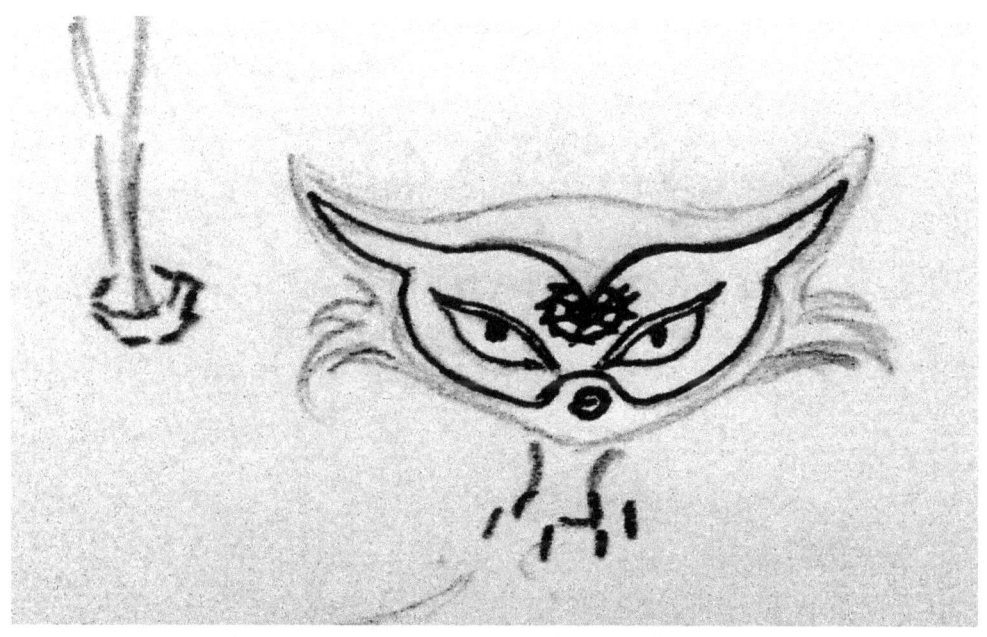

Step 4

Draw two more gears on the forehead on both sides of the previous one. Give some shading in the background of these gears. Draw some embellishments below the eyes.

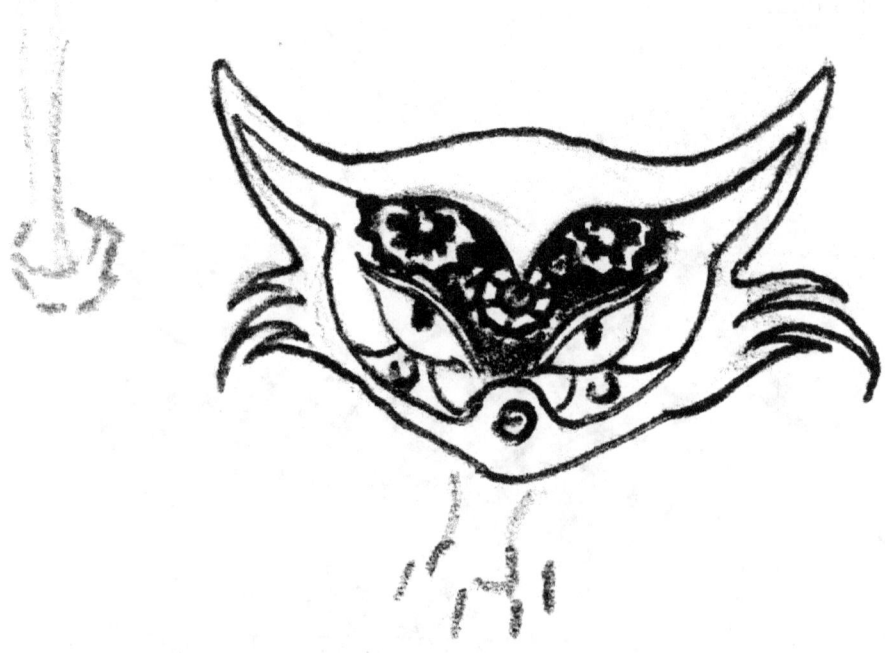

Step 5

Give shading in the rest of the face as required. Notice that a portion of the face is shaded in the form of a mask. The rest of the face is left with light shading. The eyes need not be given much detail because the mask is already there to enhance the look of the face.

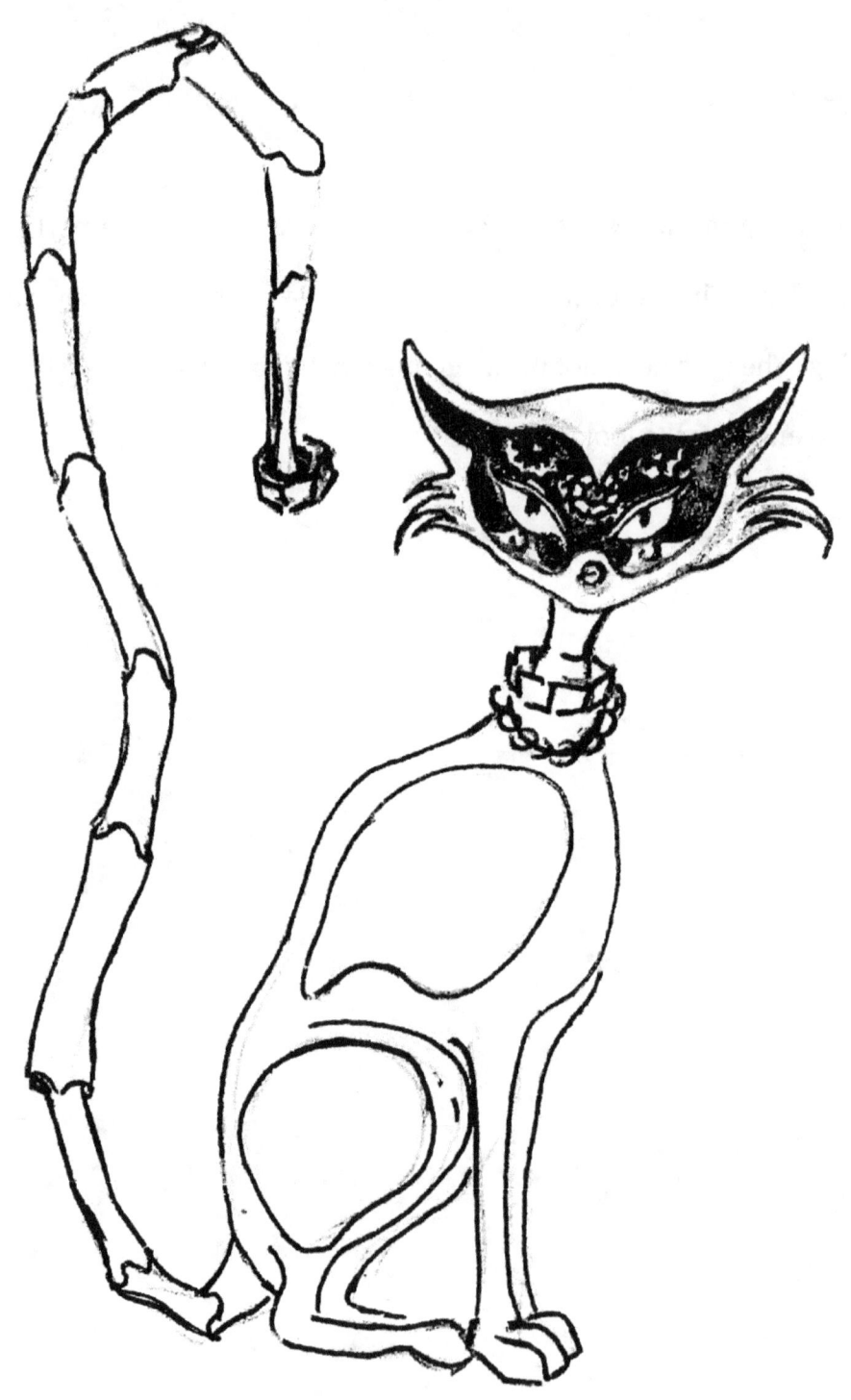

Step 6

In the upper hollow space created in the body earlier, draw a clock along with a partially visible gear. The gear is also connected to the clock with a shaft. In the second space, draw a complete gear. The teeth on the edge of this gear are also partially visible.

Draw a gear in the form of a necklace around the neck of the cat. Give a beaded necklace also in addition to the gear.

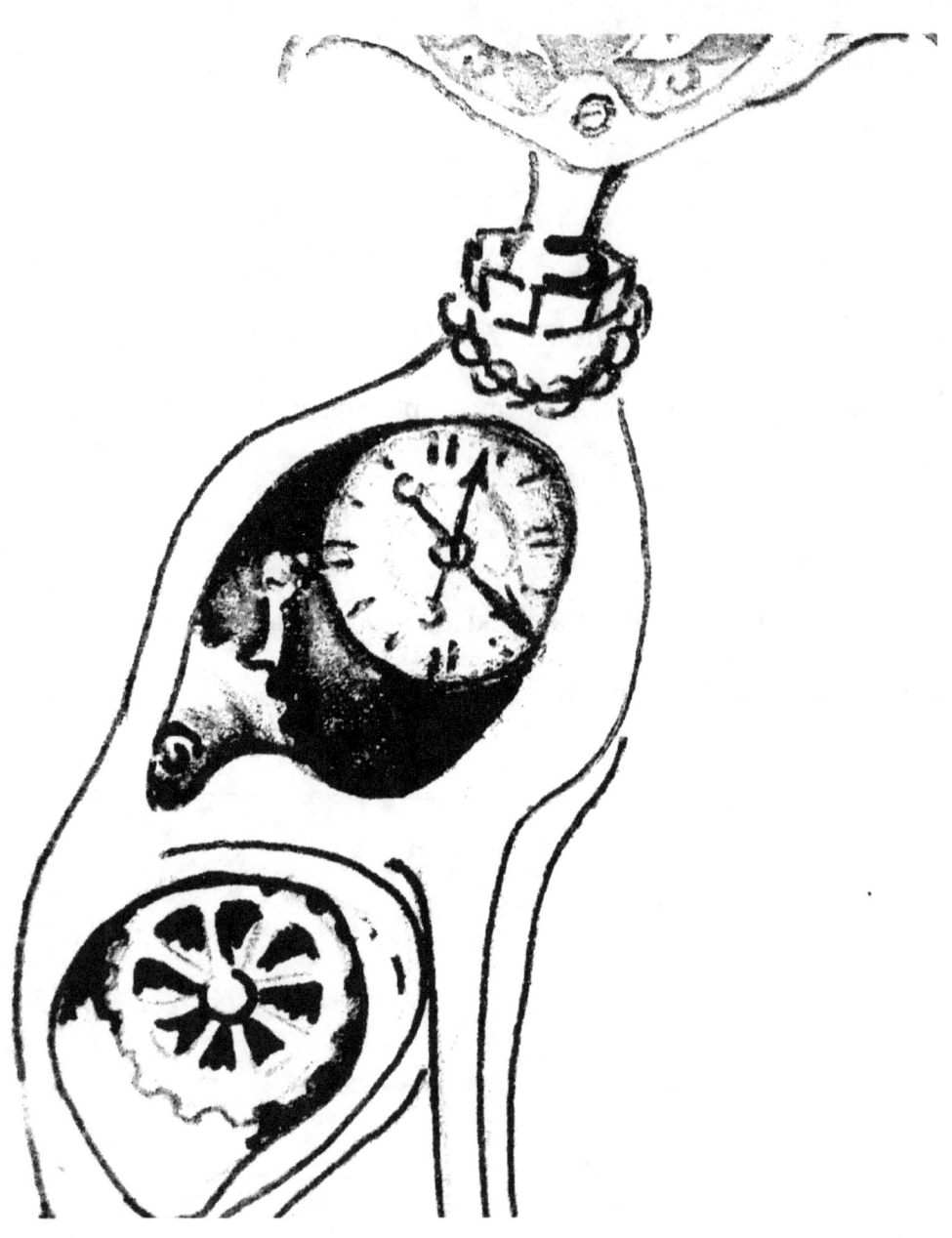

Step 7

Give light shading in the areas of neck and body around the hollow areas.

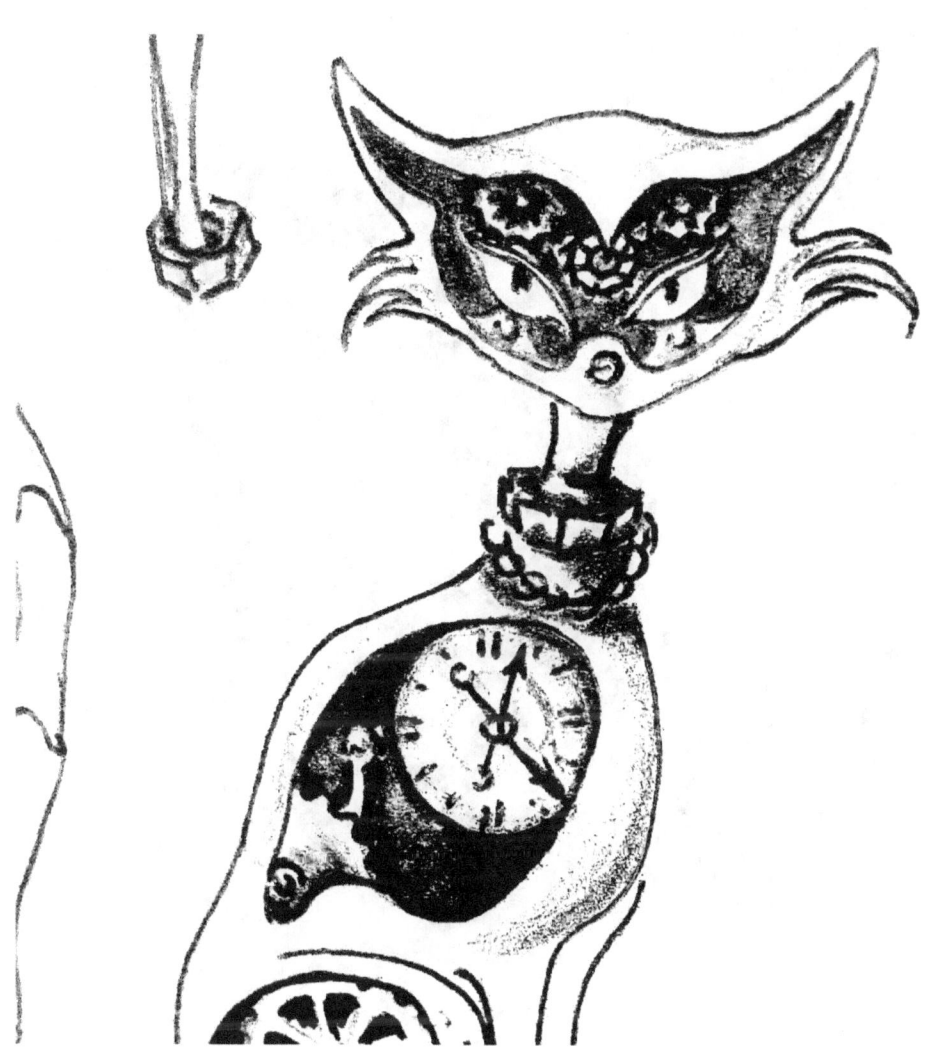

Step 8

Give shading in the legs and around the lower hollow area. Note that the two legs are partially visible because of the body posture and angle. Thus, draw and shade the legs accordingly.

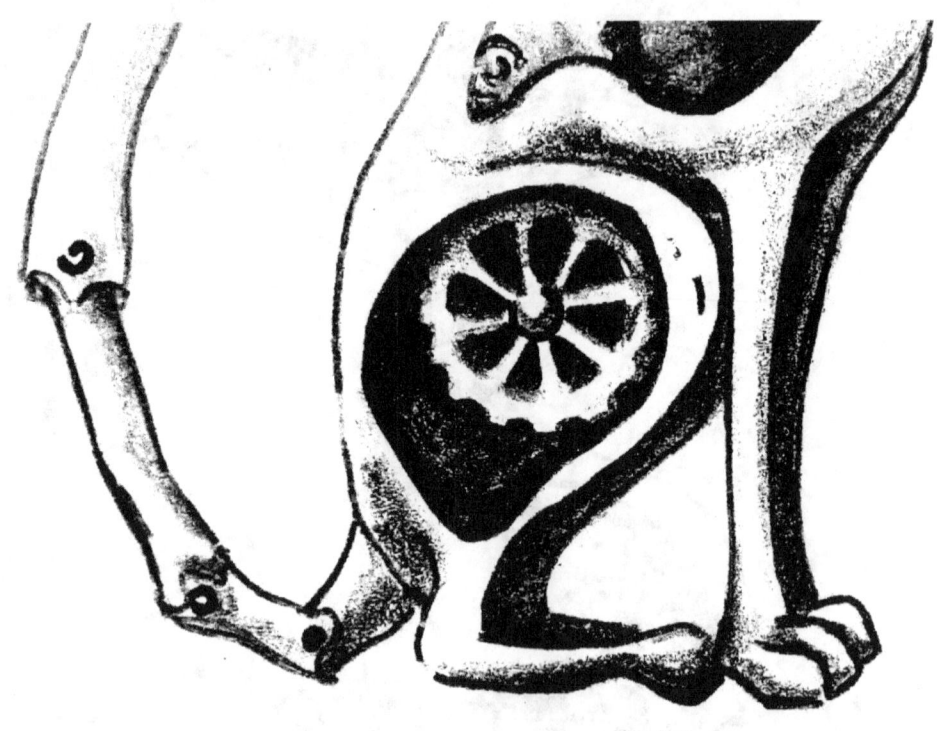

Step 9

Draw the tail of the cat with bony mechanical joints at several intervals. The joints are cojoined by the bolts. Shade the tail. The knob or rattle at the end should also be carefully shaded according to its angle.

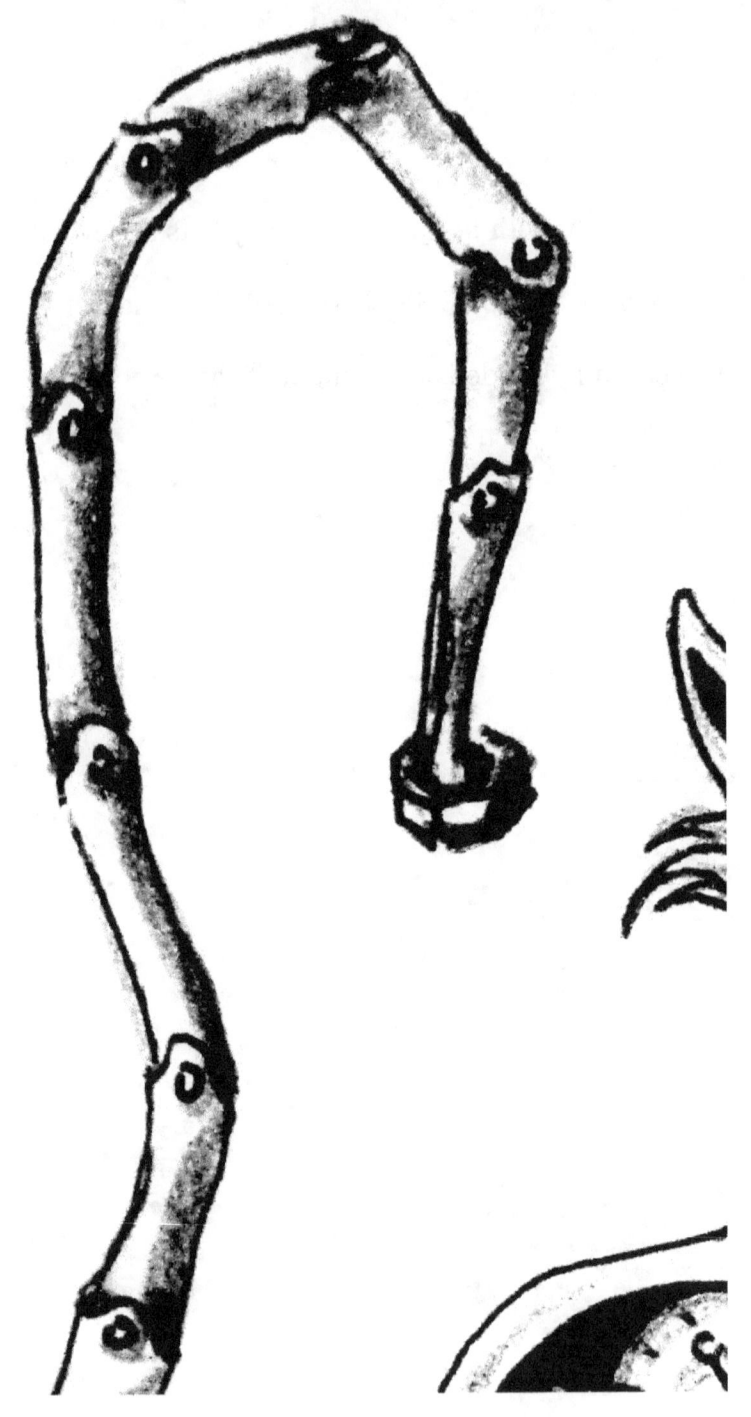

Step 10

Give finishing touches to the illustration and the Steampunk wicked cat is complete.

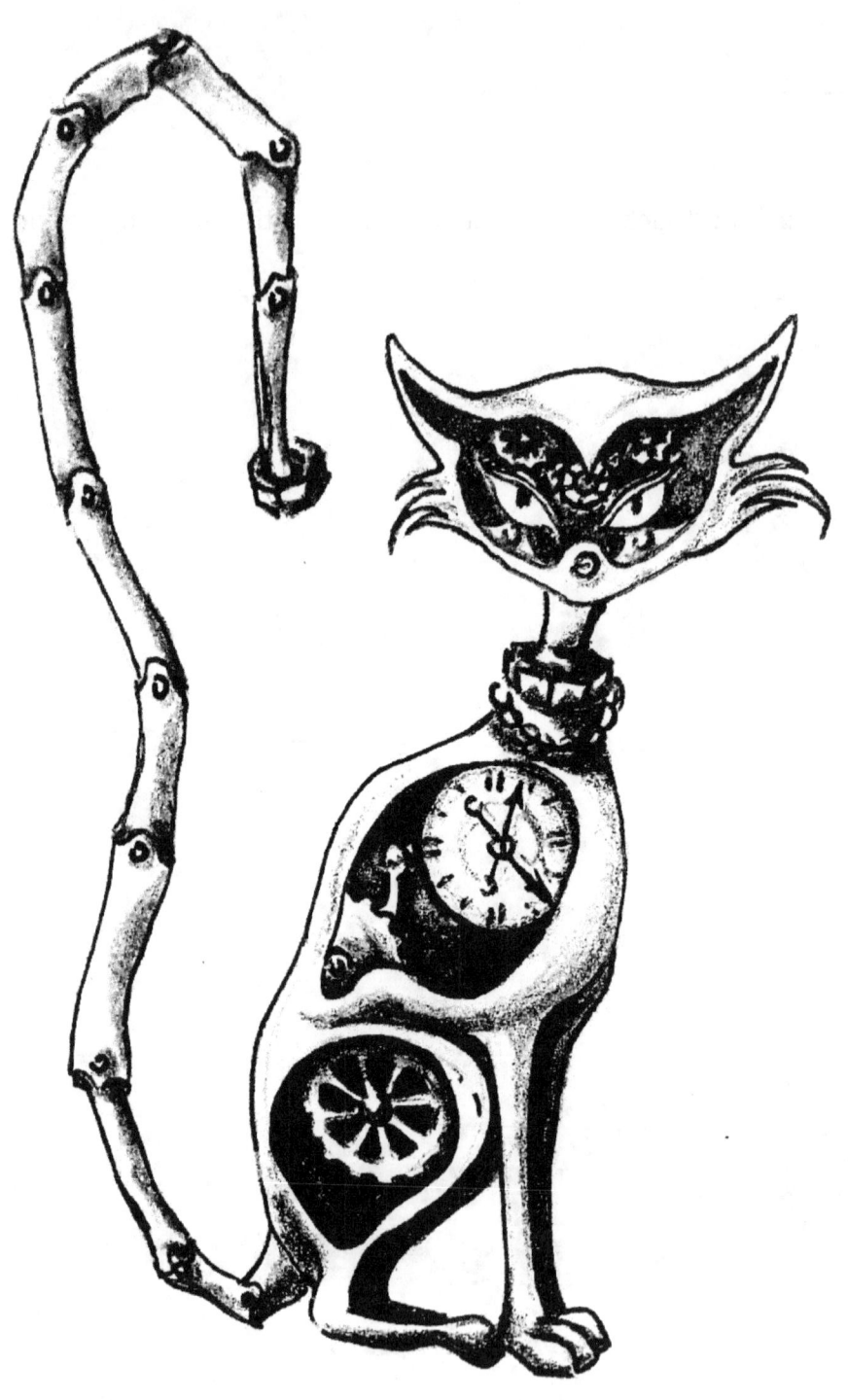

Conclusion

Now that you have read the entire book on drawing Steampunk cats, we hope that you did not face any difficulty in learning the same. **"Steampunk Cats Drawing- A Completely New Form of Cats"** has been written to introduce you to a completely new aspect of the Steampunk genre with as much ease as possible. We suggest that you read and practice more and more with this genre. The more you practice, the easier you will find to innovate. There are many things around you which you can incorporate in your drawings.

Visit your garage, for example, and look at the machinery with a completely different perspective. You will see that you can visualize something entirely different in the engine of a car than it is actually visible to the naked eye. Similarly, you might find forms of living beings in various machineries.

When you look at the Steampunk drawings already drawn by other artists, you will find many creative ideas that otherwise might not come to your mind. Take inspirations, but do not copy them. There are many ways of taking inspiration from non-Steampunk figures. You can take any regular object and convert it into a Steampunk drawing.

It is not very difficult to master this genre of Steampunk. Several machine parts such as shafts, bearings, ball bearings, fasteners, nuts, rivets, gears or cogwheels, gear trains, rack and pinion etc. become very easy to insert in any drawing if you have drawn them several times individually. You have to give sufficient time to the genre so that you can transform any picture into a Steampunk sketch.

Moreover, many apprehensions surround this genre. It is common for female artists round the world to assume that mechanical things can only be mastered by male artists only. But, the fact is that both genders have equally succeeded in the drawings and graphics of Steampunk. If you find your muse in machinery, nothing can stop you.

Other books by Jeffrey Stains

STEAMPUNK:

Drawing Amazing Steampunk Figures!
Book 1

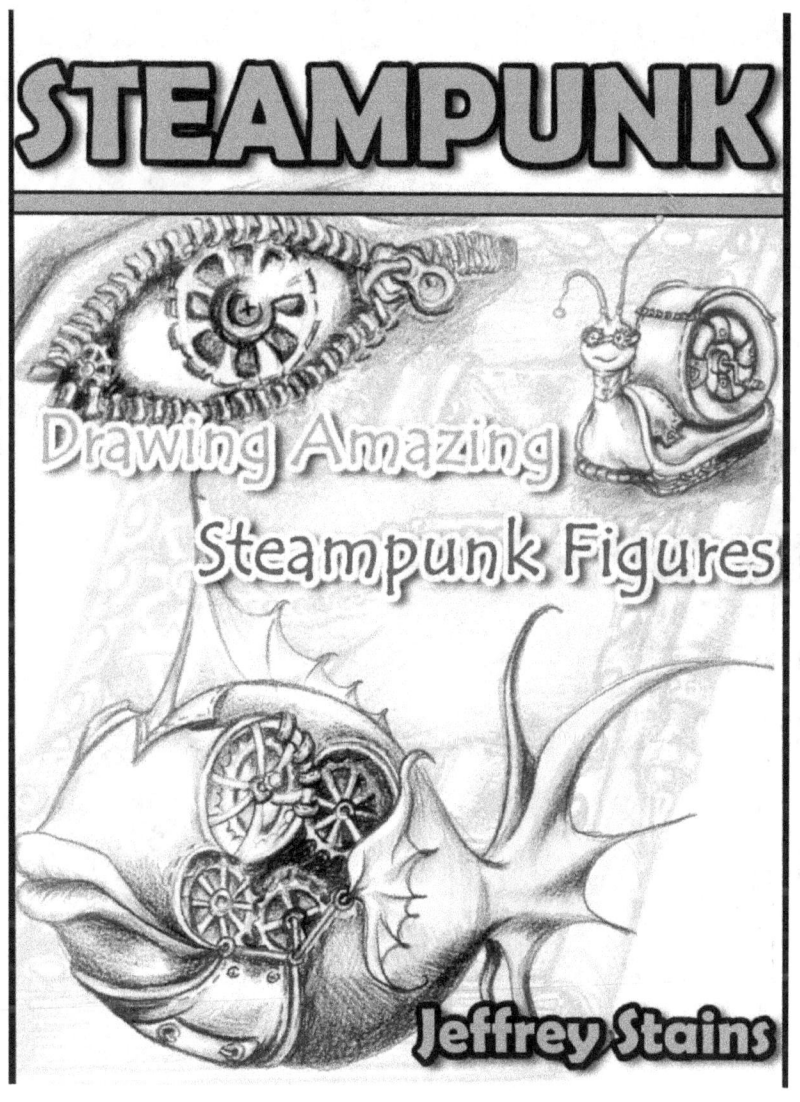

Steampunk:

Learn How to Draw
Amazing Steampunk Figures!
Book 2

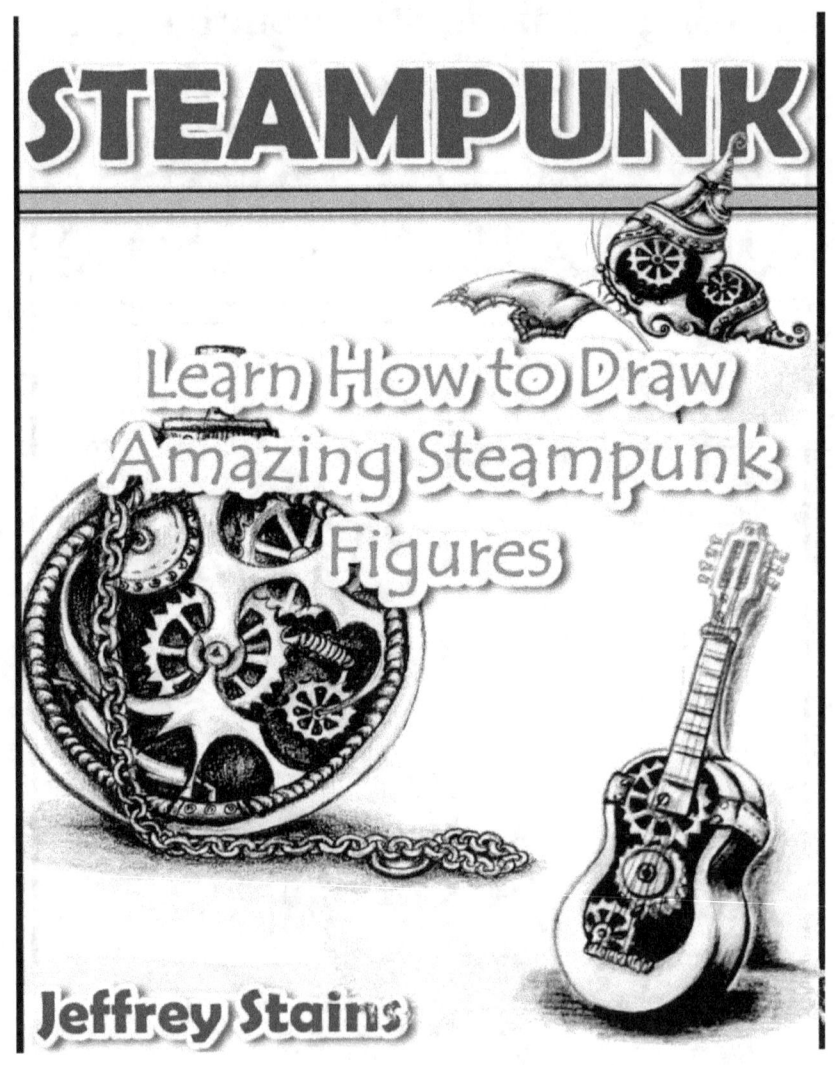

STEAMPUNK DOGS Drawing:

Unleash Your Imagination
with Creative Steampunk Dogs

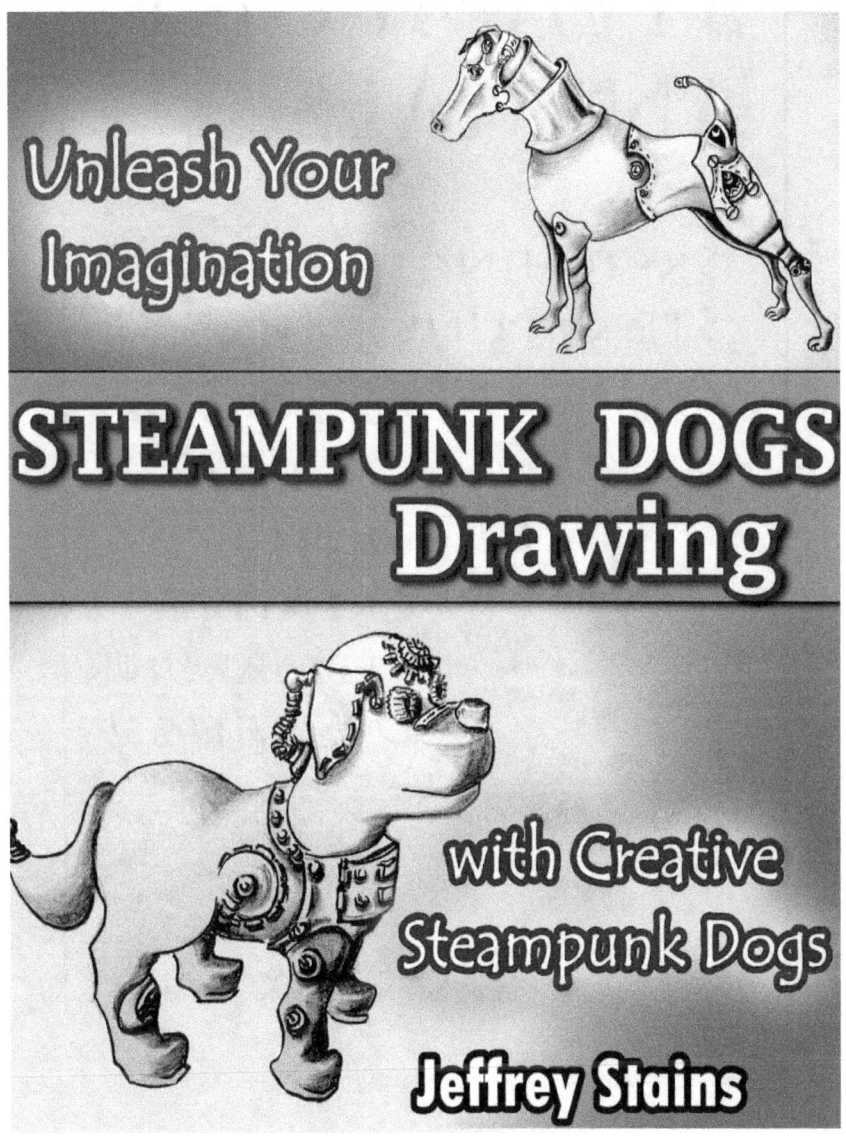

Steampunk Animals:

Sketching Steampunk Animals with Creative Steampunk Drawings!

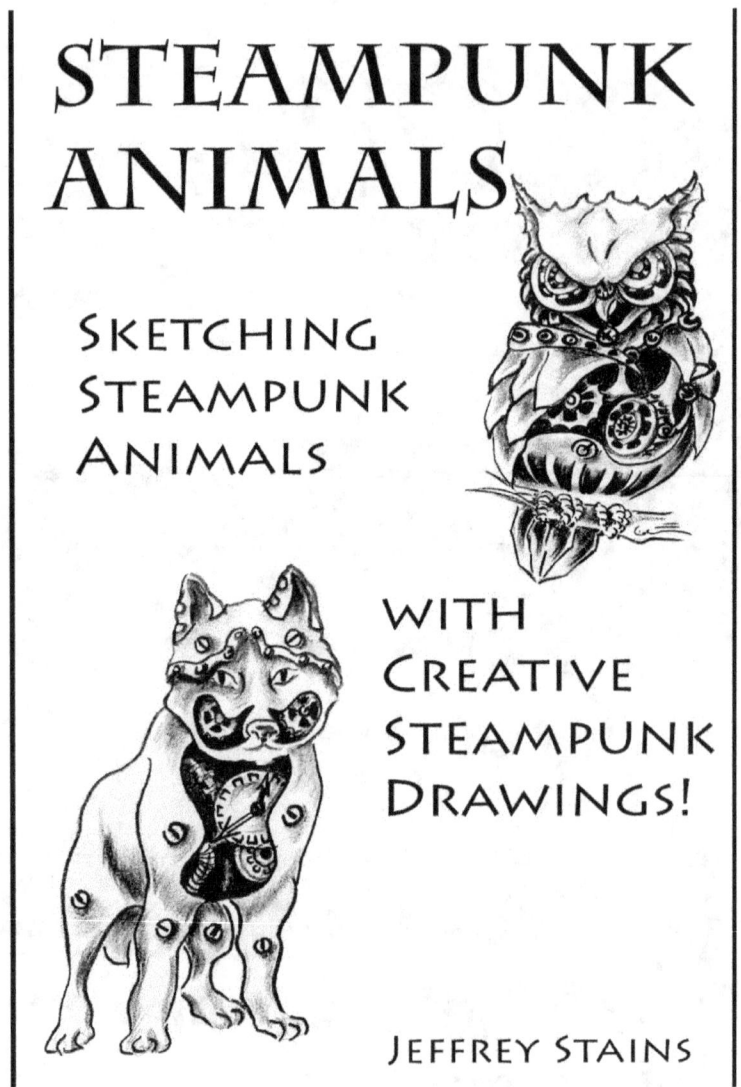

Thank you!

Thank you for choosing our book, we hope you found it interesting and helpful.

If you liked the book, please give us a favor to write your review.

We would really appreciate this!

If you would like to have a bonus – **FREE BOOK**, please send the screenshot of your review to this e-mail: **kelly.artbooks@gmail.com** and we will send you a **FREE BOOK** in PDF as a **GIFT!****

Hope to see you in our future books and good luck in your drawing experience!

** in the e-mail subject please mention the name of the book you reviewed and the author.

www.ingramcontent.com/pod-product-compliance
Lightning Source LLC
Chambersburg PA
CBHW081504170526
45166CB00008B/2553